COMPLETELY REVISED AND IMPROVED 2ND EDITION

find your voice

THE NO. 1 SINGING TUTOR

by Jo Thompson
& Nigel Nelson

for Rory and Louis

Praise for Jo Thompson:

"Jo taught me how to control my voice and hit a high note without even thinking about it. ... when I'm on the road I know what to do technically to save my voice, whereas before I wouldn't have had a clue. Working with Jo has definitely made a difference to me as an artist." **JAMES MORRISON**

"I suffered from problems with my singing voice last year and would have been lost without Jo. She is an expert at her craft and has seen my voice through a rigorous year of touring. I have a session with Jo before every big show or TV appearance to ensure my singing voice is the best it can be" **ELLY JACKSON (LA ROUX)**

"I think our tour insurers should send Jo a huge crate of vintage champagne as without her help and advice on technique and warming my voice, there is no way I could have completed all the shows I've done! She really has been a great asset to me – and she's a lovely person as well!" **CRAIG DAVID**

"I first went to Jo with a voice that I was straining and pushing, it was okay but I wasn't singing with proper technique. Now I can maintain tours and runs of extended performances with no problems – for example, I played 38 festivals this summer. I've also extended my range and tone because I can now sing clearly and with the right technique. I also suffered from crazy anxiety and Jo taught me how to relax, how to put it into my voice, to enjoy singing, and really encouraged me to do that with confidence. I've recommended loads of people to go to her and they've all come back like, 'Yeah, she's incredible'. Jo's a lovely person to be around!" **JOHN NEWMAN**

"Jo has an amazing energy and her expertise is incredible. I recommend her to every vocalist I work with." **FRASER T SMITH**

"When I came to Jo I had lost a lot of technique and ability to preserve my voice for the duration of a 45-minute show. Jo helped me build back my stamina to a level I didn't believe were possible. It's the biggest pleasure to work with Jo on such a personal level and ultimately she has enabled me to understand and trust my vocal capabilities." **ELLA EYRE**

"When I first met Jo, twenty four years ago, I was so relieved to have finally found a teacher who could relate vocal exercises and techniques to actually singing a modern pop song, plus making the process interesting and fun. We have since worked together in the studio, on film, and in the classroom with great success and become life-long friends." **KIPPER**

"Jo has been a total saving grace for me. She helped me to retrain my voice after suffering from vocal pain sustained by an injury two years ago. I went to multiple doctors before I found a solution working with Jo. She has transformed my vocal patterns and I would recommend her to any singer, particularly those who have had vocal problems." **MARINA LAMBRINI DIAMANDIS (MARINA AND THE DIAMONDS)**

"Jo is both intellectually and emotionally connected to the human voice in all its capacities from speech to song. This is why she is interesting and interested in all the nuances the voice has to offer. Jo is way ahead of the pack and this fact keeps her lessons informative and inspirational." **HEATHER SMALL**

"Jo makes everything so much easier. She has been a huge help for me, particularly with vocal endurance whilst on the road. I couldn't imagine not checking in with her pre-tour. Any anxieties – she always has the answer!" **JAMES BAY**

"Jo is a hugely talented singing coach who has encouraged me to work harder than I have ever worked before. She is a great source of inspiration." **JANE HORROCKS**

"Jo has an impressive understanding of vocal technique, phrasing and style, and her great strength is her ability to apply this effectively to rock and pop singing." **TONY HADLEY**

"Jo has helped me understand my voice so much. Not only has she strengthened my voice, she has helped me with my confidence. A brilliant teacher." **JESSIE WARE**

"I have learned many important things from Jo. She has taught me how my body and my voice work together – her visualisation techniques, for example, work unbelievably well. She has given me the confidence to relax and be natural when I perform. I think Jo was born with a gift to teach." IVE MENDES

"Jo has been our vocal coach and friend since the release of our first album. She has been a constant presence in our career since we were signed to a record label. Lots of travel, lots of touring, lots of preparation - in short, lots of singing! At times it can be vocally tiring and stressful for all of us, so it is always welcome when we get to spend time with her. From the learning of new and various techniques of using our voices to their greatest ability, to learning how to best prepare and preserve our voices for a tour, a big concert, or a 4am TV appearance, Jo always makes sure we are in the best vocal shape possible. It's a great pleasure to have Jo on our team." THE OVERTONES

"If I had to start again, knowing what I know now, then Jo Thompson would be my first and last teacher. Probably the best vocal coach in the country." STEVE HART

"I've been having singing and voice classes with Jo Thompson for several years now. Jo has a holistic approach to singing – she is not just about scales and the diaphragm. Everything is geared towards relaxation and stress-free performance. She has rightly identified that the enemy of every singer is anxiety: Will I hit the right notes? Will I be able to sing above the drums? What if my throat seizes up? Why don't I sound like Mariah Carey? (This last one is my own personal bugbear.) Jo ingeniously marries the idea of a good sing with a kind of healing thing. She pays an almost forensic attention to the different parts of your voice – the head, chest and belly. When I worked on a documentary show recently where I had to sing two songs at the Jazz Cafe for the denouement, I found Jo's daily warm ups an inspiration. Enjoy this book – it's good for your soul!" LENNY HENRY CBE

Contents

Introduction

In recent years there has been an unprecedented surge of interest in singers and singing. With the continuing popularity of karaoke and the success of wannabe pop star TV shows, more and more people want to 'have a go', many having aspirations to become professional singers in their own right.

Find Your Voice is an innovative and invaluable handbook for singers of any style or ability. The aim was to write a comprehensive and user-friendly guide that offers a practical, step-by-step course in singing technique, arranged in a logical and easy-to-follow format.

Singers of all styles and at every level will learn how to:

- develop and strengthen every aspect of their singing technique
- sing with good style and phrasing
- maximise all elements of their performance
- develop auditioning skills
- take good care of their voices, and much, much more.

The teaching of singing is still largely shrouded in mystery, and sadly many people with little real knowledge or understanding of singing have exploited this. There are far too many charlatans amongst those who put themselves forward as singing coaches. Poor, uninformed coaching ranges from the completely ineffectual to the downright damaging.

Naturally, there will always be a healthy debate amongst good practitioners about which approach is the best; indeed, there will be people who disagree with some of the things I have to say within these pages. I make no apologies for this, however.

This new, completely revised and expanded edition of *Find Your Voice* is a book born of over 25 years' experience as a singing coach and represents a personal view of singing, singers and singing training.

It is my aim to demystify what is known about the voice, explain in the clearest terms what constitutes good vocal technique, and show the best way to go about vocal training.

To anticipate the obvious question, yes, you *can* learn to be a better singer through reading a book – well, this book anyway! In fact, if you follow the basic principles and advice suggested within these pages it is my hope and anticipation that your singing will improve way beyond your expectations.

Jo Thompson

SECTION ONE:
HOW YOUR VOICE WORKS

Clearly, anyone can sing without knowing technically how their voice works – singing seems to occur quite spontaneously and naturally. However, if you *do* know something about what is happening at a physical level, it can really help your singing. Let me explain.

We all use our voices every day in a variety of ways in much the same way we drive our cars – automatically or unconsciously. It is usually only when things start to go wrong that we feel the need to look 'under the hood'.

Whilst voice production appears to be a natural part of human experience, good singing technique involves some voluntary *control* over our bodies. Consider our breathing. Like our heartbeat, most of the time we are hardly aware of the cycle of our breath. The mechanisms involved are part of our autonomic nervous system and function largely below the level of consciousness, whether we are awake or asleep.

An interesting difference between the heart and the breathing process, however, is that we can exert a degree of control over the latter. For example, we can choose to inhale and exhale quickly or slowly, and we can even hold our breath – in other words, *stop* our breathing temporarily.

As we shall see, 'correct' breathing and **support** (see page 21) are absolutely essential to good singing. One of the key principles of this book is that you need to learn to exercise a particular kind of control over your breath, and once mastered this will lead to a great improvement in your singing. In other words, there are things to learn about the use of your breath, specifically when speaking and singing, that go beyond the automatic 'ebb and flow' of normal breathing.

There are, then, several *physical* elements to singing, including breathing and support, over which a singer must learn to gain some control, and, put together, these constitute what we refer to as **technique**.

In order to understand how to sing well I believe it really helps to have a little anatomical knowledge, since it provides a framework on which you can hang everything else you learn about your voice.

So, although the thought of a quick biology lesson might switch some of you off, I strongly urge you to take the trouble to read this section because, if you do, everything that follows will make a lot more sense. In addition, there are a number of exercises I recommend here that will help you get in touch with the parts of your body you should be using when you sing.

The first two chapters in the section, *Breath* and *Vocal Cords*, deal with how the basic singing sound is produced and, from the singer's point of view, the most effective way to go about this. The key concept of *Support* is discussed here. There then follows a chapter on the *Larynx* and one on the *Mouth*, in which the importance of the tongue, jaw, soft palate and pharynx is explained.

Throughout the book reference is made to the kinds of problems some people experience with their voices. Voice care and voice health are extremely important concerns. I would argue strongly that if you know a little about what can go wrong physically with your voice, it can be a lot easier to put things right – or better still avoid developing problems in the first place.

Chapter 1
Breath

Without breath – well, let's face it, you wouldn't be reading this now! Seriously though, breathing properly and supporting the breath correctly is the key to singing well. Without air, of course, there's no sound. Let's start by looking closely at what happens to the breath and how the sound is created.

The Cycle Of Breath

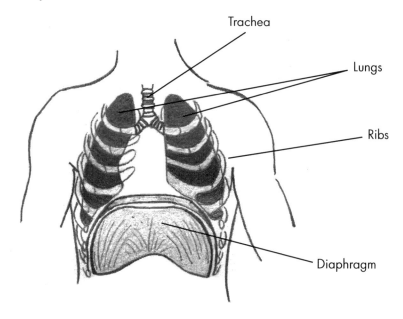

Trachea

Lungs

Ribs

Diaphragm

Breathing In

As you inhale, air travels in through your nose or mouth, through your larynx (voice box), down your trachea (windpipe) and into the lungs. Your lungs and the ribcage that surrounds them expand – you can imagine yourself as a balloon filling with air.

Breathing Out

As you breathe out, the air flows from your lungs, back up through your trachea, through your larynx and out through your nose or mouth. It is when the air is flowing back through your larynx that the sound is produced. Your vocal cords (or vocal *folds*) are inside this 'box' and as the air, under pressure, passes over them they vibrate and it is this that creates the sound. (See *Vocal Cords*, page 25)

The Diaphragm

The diaphragm is a large, strong, dome-shaped muscle separating your heart and lungs from the rest of your 'insides'. It is the main muscle involved in breathing. The diaphragm is joined to your sternum (breastbone) at the front and to your spine at the back. The diaphragm works like a bellows – the rise-and-fall motion of the diaphragm fills and empties air from the lungs.

When you breathe in your diaphragm flattens out. As it does so it 'squashes' down onto your other organs and pushes your abdomen out. Similarly, as you breathe out it moves back up.

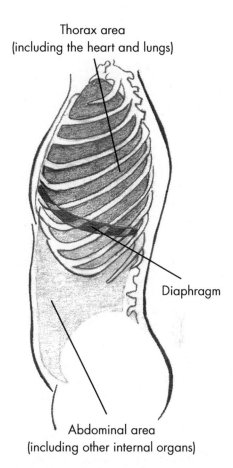

Thorax area
(including the heart and lungs)

Diaphragm

Abdominal area
(including other internal organs)

Gaining Control Over Your Breathing

To begin to develop any control over your singing it is essential to develop an understanding and awareness of your breathing: how it feels to breathe deeply, and how it feels to control this deep breath in the most effective way.

To achieve a smooth, flowing sound you require smooth-flowing breath. You have to be able to control the out-flow of air as you are singing so that you don't use it up all in one go. You must learn how to release the breath gradually in order to control the sound and be able to sustain any length of phrase. This control of the breath is known as **support**, which we shall be looking at in detail later.

You might think that there is only one way of breathing, but in fact you can breathe in different ways. These variations can be categorized as *clavicular, intercostal* and *diaphragmatic*. As I will explain, *diaphragmatic* breathing is the type of breathing you should be developing – the other two should be avoided. Let me explain why.

Clavicular Breathing

Clavicular breathing means breathing into your clavicles or collarbones. If your breathing is centred here, you will feel it high up in your chest. It will be shallow and feel 'snatched' or 'grasped'. You will also feel tight across your chest and shoulders, and this will be reflected in your singing. Incidentally, this is where you breathe when you are in panic mode. Clearly, if you are feeling anxious when you sing you can find yourself in a vicious circle of constantly snatching in breath, which in turn fuels the feeling of panic.

Intercostal Breathing

The ribcage contains the lungs and consists of twelve pairs of ribs. All of them can move, except for the first pair. The intercostal muscles connect the ribs to each other. As you breathe in the external intercostals lift the ribs and allow more space for your lungs to fill with air. As you breathe out the internal intercostals pull the ribs back down.

Some singing teachers encourage this way of breathing. Whilst it is true the intercostals play a part in controlling the diaphragm as you breathe out, I think focusing on these muscles is a mistake. I was taught this approach and encouraged to practice singing with my hands on the sides of my ribcage. It created a huge amount of tension in my body which was then transferred to my singing. I therefore do not recommend it.

Diaphragmatic Breathing

The diaphragm is the most active and important muscle involved in breathing. The fall-and-rise action of the diaphragm fills and empties air from the lungs.

As you breathe in, the diaphragm and intercostal muscles contract together, enlarging the chest wall and allowing the lungs to expand with air. When you breathe out, the ribs and diaphragm relax, the chest wall goes back to its normal position and the air is squeezed out. Simultaneously, the deep abdominal muscles, especially the transversus abdominis, contract to help with the release of the air.

There are three layers to the abdominal muscles: from the outside moving in, the rectus abdominis and external obliques, then the internal obliques, and finally the transversus abdominis. It is the deepest muscle layer, the transversus abdominis,

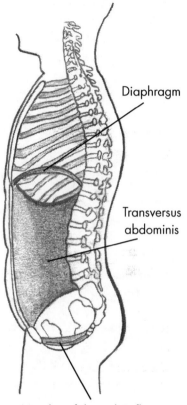

Diaphragm

Transversus abdominis

Muscles of the pelvic floor

lying under the other two, which is the one you want to be in touch with. The transversus abdominis is often referred to as your 'core muscle'. Those of you who do Pilates or work out in the gym are likely to be aware of it. It is attached to the diaphragm and is the third layer of muscle in (see the diagram below). When you engage it there is a feeling of internal control, but this should not be experienced as pushing, squeezing or forcing. The transversus abdominis (or transverse abdominus as it is also known) is not to be confused with what people refer to as their 'abs' (the 'six pack'), the more external rectus abdominis. In efficient diaphragmatic breathing you engage the transversus abdominis and not the more external muscles.

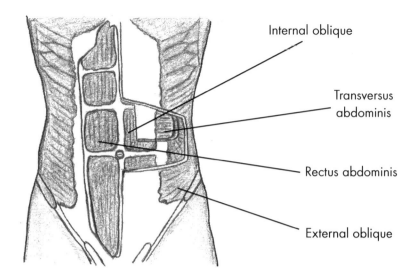

Internal oblique

Transversus
abdominis

Rectus abdominis

External oblique

Here is a good exercise to help you connect with the transversus abdominis.
If you do the exercise correctly you will begin to understand what I mean by
diaphragmatic breathing.

> *Stand with your feet the width of your hips apart. Put your hands below your*
> *tummy button. Breathe out slowly whilst gently drawing your tummy button*
> *backwards towards your spine.*

And here's another good exercise to connect with this muscle.

> *Stand with your feet the width of your hips apart. Put your hands below your*
> *tummy button. Breathe out in short bursts, making a 'vv' sound. Your tummy*
> *should feel like it is 'springing' in with each out-breath. Repeat several times.*
> *Slide up and down in pitch on the 'vv', it feels a bit like you are softly revving*
> *a car engine. It doesn't want to be loud or forced.*

You want to feel this muscular connection when singing. This muscle needs
to be permanently 'switched on', although you will have to consciously engage
it more at particular times. For example, when you sing a high or sustained
note you need greater control over your breath, so you increase the muscle

engagement. This is at the root of what we call **support** (see page 20) which we will move on to after we have done some work on our breathing.

The more you practice controlling your breath in the right way, the more natural it will feel and the easier your singing will become. When you are supporting your voice well, you may feel the muscles in your lower back beginning to work. This will happen naturally. Don't try to force them to work as it can create tension in your breath and body.

Never adopt any breathing practices which feel awkward or uncomfortable. The breath should always feel relaxed. If something really doesn't feel comfortable don't do it!

Note: Many dancers have been trained to pull their tummies in as they breathe in. They therefore find it difficult to adjust to the idea that when you breathe in to sing, your tummy should move out.

Mental Control

Because it can be hard to imagine what is happening to the muscles involved in breathing, developing some mental imagery will help you achieve or 'anchor' the kind of control you want. For example, I never think of pushing *out* sound or breath; instead I think about drawing it *in* (where I gain control of it). By 'thinking' about it – focusing or directing your thoughts into particular areas – you can alter the places where you feel the breath and where the sound resonates.

Breathing Exercises

Some voice teachers are not big fans of breathing exercises, but I believe they are an essential way of getting in touch with your breathing, feeling its natural rhythm and experiencing its full potential.

Most of my examples have their roots in Hatha Yoga breathing practices.

Breathing exercises are also a very useful tool for relaxation. They change how you feel both physically and mentally. I use them a lot to help singers steady their nerves before a live gig or TV performance. Many performers (including sportsmen and women) feel extremely anxious before they go out to perform – a mixture of nerves and excess adrenalin – and some are even physically sick. Spending time breathing will help you get into the right frame of mind to be as focused as possible to get the most out of your performance.

Exercises

1. Three-stage Breathing

I love this yoga breathing exercise. It is incredibly relaxing and helps you become more profoundly aware of you breathing.

Lie on the floor with your knees bent and your feet flat on the floor, with your head resting on two medium-sized paperbacks. Rest your hands on your tummy, just below your tummy button. Breathe in and out through your nose, but if you find this difficult breathe in through your mouth. Relax and consciously slow down your breathing. Picture the bottom of your lungs filling with air as you breathe in. If your mind starts to wander bring it back to your breathing. Do this for 12 breaths.

Next, move your hands into the middle of your tummy. Picture the middle of your lungs filling with air and feel your ribcage at the front, sides and back moving in to the floor. Again, repeat for 12 breaths.

Now place your hands on your collarbones. Use the in-breath to help you open up across your chest and shoulders. Use the out-breath, which is the 'relaxing' breath, to let go of tension. As singers we are always trying to avoid breathing here but it feels good to open up this area.

Finally, place your hands back on your lower tummy and breathe using the whole of your lungs. As you breathe in, picture filling your lungs from the bottom up, and as you breathe out empty them from the top down. You can visualise this as a wave of breath washing in and out, or it could be a nice, warm colour filling your lungs.

2. Counting Breath

This exercise has a calming effect, leaving your mind and body feeling 'quiet'. Use the thought of breath being 'quiet' to help you avoid gasping in air before you sing.

Part 1: Lie on the floor as in Exercise 1. Slowly breathe out through your nose. Note that in all the exercises so far you have been breathing in through your nose, not your mouth. Breathing through the nose is more relaxing and makes it easier to get the breath into the bottom of your lungs. When you sing you have to take air in through your mouth as there isn't time to take it in through your nose.

Slow your breathing down. Breathe out for a slow count of 5 or 6 and then in slowly for the same count. Don't force anything; the length of breath can be longer or shorter.

Part 2: Repeat Part 1. Breathe out then pause for the same count before breathing in.

Part 3: Repeat Part 2, but this time, after you have breathed in, pause for the same count and then breathe out again. So the pattern is: breathe out, pause, breathe in, pause. Never strain the breath; do what feels ok for you.

Always start with the out-breath as this is the relaxing phase of the breathing; when you pause, your body becomes extremely still and relaxed.

3. Humming Bee Breath

This exercise is helpful in observing the steadiness of your airflow.

Sit or kneel comfortably. Put your fingers on your ears – on the bit just above your lobes which when pressed covers the openings of your ears. Hum a note (not too high) on an 'mmm' sound, with your lips lightly touching. You should feel the note vibrating around your nose and the front of your face, or in your chest (or a bit of both). The sound will resemble that of a buzzing bee. Because your ears are covered, the sound will be louder and more buzzy in your head.

> *Notice how long the breath lasts. Is it shaky? Does it come in waves? With practice you can make the sound even. To start with, try practicing for two minutes and gradually increase it to five minutes. You can experiment with varying the pitch of the note, taking it a little higher or lower. If you practice this in a group you can create some amazing harmonies and clusters of sound.*

You will find doing this exercise incredibly relaxing – for the body, voice and mind.

4.   Getting In Touch With Your Diaphragm

I use this exercise to get in touch with my diaphragm ready for singing. It is very similar to the previous exercise on 'vv' and helps you connect with your transversus abdominis. As you do the exercise you can imagine the sound spreading down and out onto a big platform surrounding your pelvic floor. I imagine a 'skirt' about a metre in diameter that the breath almost 'sits' on. I often refer to this as a 'Cinderella dress'.

> *You can do this exercise standing, kneeling or sitting (either cross-legged or on a chair). If standing, have your feet the width of your hips apart. Spread your bodyweight evenly. Put your hands below your tummy button. Make a 'ssh' sound, letting out the breath in short bursts. Continue for the length of the breath. The in-breath will then happen spontaneously. When you feel ready repeat the exercise. If you are getting dizzy, stop.*

Breathing For Singing

Working on the exercises will give you a feel for how you should be breathing when you sing. Avoid snatching or gasping in air. Keep your chest and shoulders relaxed. Always keep the feeling of breath low and relaxed and let it flow smoothly.

It is when you come to sing, however, that things can suddenly go a bit pear-shaped. You might start out okay, but the more you sing, the harder you may find it to keep the breath low enough. If this is happening, you will be gasping air in a shallow way. As we have seen, you need to anchor the breath by engaging your transversus abdominis. Remember you feel this by drawing your tummy button in towards your spine. (You will find more about how to use your breath specifically when singing a song in the *Breathing Within A Song* section on page 92.)

Having identified the correct way of breathing, it is now time to look more closely at *how* to control the breath when singing. This vitally important control of the breath is known as *support*.

Support

Nearly every singer or singing teacher will give you a different description of what support is and how best to achieve it. Everyone agrees, however, it is about the control of air as you sing, and that it is absolutely fundamental to any singing technique. Without control of the breath you will lack control over length of phrase, tone, resonance, range, dynamics – the lot!

The correct way of supporting involves the slowing down or control of the *inward* movement of the abdominal muscles as you breathe out (which, of course, thereby controls the movement of the diaphragm). Remember, as you breathe in, your diaphragm flattens out and your abdominal muscles move out. As you breathe out, your diaphragm comes back up and your abdominal muscles move back in. This way of supporting is totally in tune with the way your breathing system naturally works.

A few singing teachers still advocate pushing out as you breathe out – the aim being to resist the upward movement of the diaphragm. This way of supporting tends to be more of a male thing as it is very physical (although some women do practice it). I was taught a version of this method and it didn't work for me. In fact, as a result, I ended up singing with a huge amount of tension in my body.

In my experience, if you do 'push out' it is very easy to put pressure on your vocal cords and strain your voice – as well as over-tensing other parts of your body. You are working too much against nature. After all, the natural way is for your tummy or abdomen to come in as you breathe out. I want to emphasise the method of support I believe in works equally well for both men and women.

Many people are under the misapprehension that you need to have very strong 'abs' in order to control the diaphragm. This is, however, not the case. As we have seen, there are three layers of abdominal muscles. Starting from the outside are the rectus abdominis and exterior obliques, under these are the interior obliques, and then finally the transversus abdominis. It is the latter muscle, deepest in the body, that controls the movement of the diaphragm. This muscle is very large and is connected to the diaphragm – at the top to the ribs and at the bottom to the pubic bone. It is a sort of diamond shape.

There should be no squeezing or forcing when you control the breath. The control should be experienced as a subtle form of sustained muscular engagement in the internal abdominal muscle (the transversus abdominis) as you breathe out, but not a rigid one. If you over exert with the external and internal oblique muscles you will put too much pressure on your larynx and vocal cords. When you start a phrase you need to engage the muscles so that they are ready to work. This could be described as a 'pull in', gently drawing your tummy button back towards your spine.

Support can also be thought of as a *springiness* in the lower abdomen as you breathe out. Once you have engaged the transversus abdominis you need to exert control over it otherwise you will lose control of the breath. Every single phrase should be supported from the start and this support continued evenly throughout. If you do the following exercise things will become clearer.

Repeat the exercise on page 20 (in the section on diaphragmatic breathing), putting your hands on your tummy, breathing out on a 'vv' sound. With each 'vv' your tummy should 'spring' in. It does this naturally as a result of the air coming out. When you are supporting your voice properly you feel this engagement.

When you are singing and supporting the sound, you consciously have to make this 'spring' happen.

Now repeat the exercise, letting the breath out as slowly as you can.

Do the exercise again but now get louder and softer. When you get louder you should feel the muscular engagement more. It is this kind of continuous sustained engagement you should be feeling when you are supporting your singing.

There are times, however, when you will need a bit of extra support – for example, if you are singing long or high notes or a sustained phrase. Here I think of engaging my whole body with the sound. I imagine a feeling of downward springiness and energy, the sound spreading on the platform of supported air. I always imagine the sound moving down, opening out, cruising on the platform of my pelvic floor as I open out in my chest and shoulders. It is a very physical feeling.

I find visualisation of the support extremely helpful; for example, I use a combination of thinking down and open. I imagine I am grabbing hold of two large stretchy resistance bands (like those used in gyms). Starting by holding them in front of my face I stretch them down inside me below my tummy button. This really gives me a sense of drawing the sound into my body. Once the sound is in I think about opening it up, for example by using the 'Cinderella dress' image (see page 20).

Don't exert too much pressure though, as you may tighten the muscles of your larynx and put too much strain on your vocal cords – you could also push out all the air in one go. As a general rule, I don't like any 'techniques' which involve too much squeezing, pulling, pushing etc.

There is another crucial element to support. This is the role of the **larynx**. It is very important that you keep a low, relaxed larynx when you sing. This does not mean you forcibly push your larynx down. Again, this is achieved by mental control.

The 'straw' exercise in Chapter 3 (see page 31) is very effective in helping you connect to your support as well as relaxing the muscles of your larynx. It is one of the best exercises around.

In my view, support is achieved through working the muscles that control the breath in the way I have described, whilst simultaneously maintaining a low, relaxed larynx. (See *Keeping A Low Larynx*, page 30)

To help you achieve this, visualise having a big, round tube or column the width of your body that reaches from the back of your throat right down into your body. Think of your larynx as a weight that 'leans' down into this space. Try to imagine pushing a beach ball under water as you sing. If you push the ball down, its buoyancy will push it back up again and the ball will come out of the water. You have to keep pushing the ball (or the sound) down against the diaphragm, which is coming up. It is a feeling of compression.

As I sing I imagine this downward movement combined with the feeling of the support. The sound spreads onto and 'cruises' on a massive platform of supported air.

When you have both these elements working together, the feeling is one of your whole body being involved in making the sound, and the results are exhilarating!

Chapter 2
The Vocal Cords

What Are They?

Let's get something right first: you spell them *cords* (as in rope) not *chords* (as in a group of musical notes). They are also referred to as the 'vocal folds' or 'true' vocal folds. This is the term used by doctors and speech therapists and is a better description of what they really are.

People have all sorts of strange ideas about what the vocal cords look like – and how many there are. Well, to put the record straight, we have just two of them, and they reach from the front to the back of the larynx or 'voice box' (see diagrams below and those in the section on the *Larynx* in Chapter 3). They are attached to the thyroid cartilage, the front of which is known as the Adam's Apple. This 'thyroid cartilage' is hard and protects the cords.

The cords lie stretched across the trachea (or windpipe) and, as the air passes out through the lungs, it passes over the cords (which have been drawn together); they vibrate and the sound is produced. Think how you can make a squealing noise by blowing through blades of grass held together between your thumbs; the process is similar.

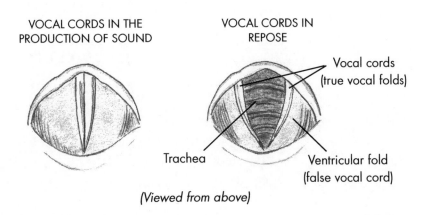

VOCAL CORDS IN THE
PRODUCTION OF SOUND

VOCAL CORDS IN
REPOSE

Vocal cords
(true vocal folds)

Trachea

Ventricular fold
(false vocal cord)

(Viewed from above)

Note: There is, in fact, another pair of cords or folds. They lie above and parallel to the true cords. These help to protect the vocal cords. When you swallow they come together to make a firm valve or seal. They are not normally involved in making sound, but for some people, particularly those with voice problems, they do come into play, often resulting in a muffled, throaty sound.

Incidentally, in the eighteenth century, Antoine Ferrein, one of the first people to study vocal physiology, conducted an experiment to investigate how the larynx produced sound. His experiment involved using the larynx of a dead dog – nice. He pulled the vocal cords together and blew into the trachea. To his delight a sound was produced. This is one way of remembering that, with the help of this book, there is now no excuse for singing like a dog.

Your vocal cords are highly elastic and have a very complex structure, being made up of different types of tissue and muscle fibres. They are always closed at the front and open like a 'V' at the back.

KEY POINT

The actual singing sound is created by the vocal cords or folds, which vibrate as the out-breath passes over them

When you are not making any sound, your vocal cords remain quite slack. The opening between the cords is called the 'chink of the glottis'. When you sing, the cords are brought close together and the 'chink' disappears. Depending on how low or high you are singing, more or less of the cords vibrate. When you sing a low note the cords are pulled together and the whole mass vibrates.

Gradually, as you sing higher, the 'tension' on your cords is increased as they are pulled more taut and, as a result, less of the cords vibrate. When you sing a high note only the inside edges of the cords are vibrating. Think how the pitch of a guitar string is altered. You raise the pitch by tightening the string, and lower the pitch by slackening it off.

Remember, this is only the start – we are still only talking at the level of basic sound production. Once the raw sound is produced it is what you *do* with it that is important and defines the sound you want to make and the kind of singer you will be. There is, in fact, a huge amount you can do with the raw sound and this will be covered in Section Three.

Unfortunately, various nasty things can develop on and around your cords if you don't look after them: nodules, cysts, polyps and burst blood vessels. If you learn to use your voice properly and avoid the kind of straining, which, as I will explain, can harm your voice, you stand a good chance of being spared such problems. It is worth mentioning, though, that apart from straining your voice through singing, the commonest cause of voice strain is excessive shouting – whether it be at football games, concerts, loud music venues or during post-gig socializing!

Heavy use of the speaking voice can also be damaging – many schoolteachers, for example, experience real voice problems. If you have a cough or throat infection, persistent voice use can also cause damage. For more information on these kinds of problems and what to do about them, read the section *Maintenance, Breakdown and Recovery* (page 171).

Chapter 3
The Larynx

The larynx, or voice box, is situated at the top of the trachea (windpipe) and below the pharynx (back wall of the throat). It is a kind of a V-shaped box made of cartilage, joined by ligaments, membranes and muscles, and it contains the vocal cords. The 'sharp' end of it points forward and sticks out in the throat.

It feels a little odd, and some people can't bear doing this, but you can actually move your larynx around using your fingers.

> *Rest one hand either side of your neck, in line with your Adam's Apple and gently move your larynx from side to side. It feels quite strange as it is suspended from your hyoid or tongue bone.*

The larynx is very important to us and does a number of jobs. At the top of it, at the back, is your epiglottis. This is a 'flap' of cartilage that closes off the larynx when you are eating or drinking to prevent you from choking. The larynx also acts as an air passage as well as housing your vocal cords.

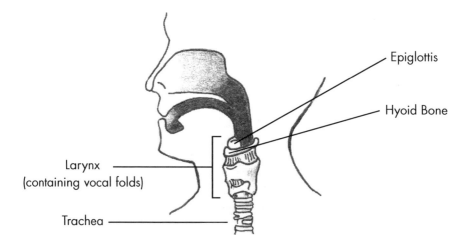

Epiglottis

Hyoid Bone

Larynx
(containing vocal folds)

Trachea

The larynx is incredibly muscular. Some muscles lift the larynx and some lower it. The sternocleidomastoids (phew!) are some we don't want to see in action at all. These are the large ones at the side of the neck which stand out when singers are straining. Invariably, these people will be singing with an extremely high larynx.

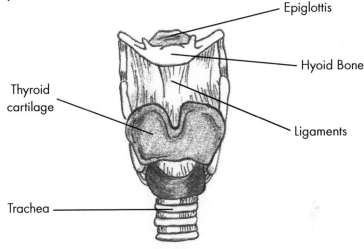

THE LARYNX *(front view)*

What happens when you sing high notes?

Rest your hands gently on your larynx. Sing a low note and join it to a high note. Can you feel your larynx move up?

Tilting The Larynx

This is something that generally happens quite naturally as you sing higher. The larynx consists of three main cartilages (the *thyroid, cricoid* and *arytenoids*). The *thyroid* cartilage sits on top of the *cricoid* cartilage) and they are connected to each other via a muscle (*the cricothyroid*). When this muscle contracts it pulls the thyroid slightly forward and down; this then tilts the thyroid. By bringing the thyroid cartilage forward and downwards, tension is placed on the vocal cords and it allows a higher pitched sound to be produced. There is more tension in the vocal cords as they are stretched. The more stretched they are, the higher the sound.

It is easier to sing higher notes if this tilt happens. However, many singers get very confused about this tilt and try to do all sorts of strange things to make it happen. If you put your hand gently on your larynx and pretend to sob you can feel this movement. You really only need to be aware of it if you're singing high in head voice, but even then I think a simple thought of the sound coming up and over from the back of the head, over the top to the front of the face, allows this to happen naturally. Alternatively, think of the sound being a slim channel above the front of your head that drops into the front of your face behind your eyes as you sing higher.

Keeping A Low Larynx

Many singers experience tightness in their throats as they sing high notes. Well, as I have mentioned, some of the muscles inside your larynx will help you to keep it low and relaxed. Obviously, you can't 'grab hold' of these muscles to feel them working together; you get them to do what you want through mental control.

It's not as hard as it sounds. Every time you sing higher, think 'down' (but don't reverse it and think 'up' as you sing down). As you sing, use mental pictures to help you: think of an elevator plunging down in its shaft; a cafetière being pushed down; a see-saw going down as the singing comes up. You may find these helpful or you may come up with your own images; different things resonate with different people. It is surprising how much these mental images can change the feeling of the singing.

KEY POINT

It is essential to keep a low, relaxed larynx when singing. This is achieved by using mental imagery and control.

Never try to 'force' your larynx down – this will create unwanted tension. Avoid pushing down with the back of your tongue. The aim is to keep your larynx in a relaxed position while singing. Visualising or feeling the relaxation of the larynx when you sing is key.

As the larynx is attached (via the sternothyroid and sternohyoid muscles) to the sternum (breastbone), another very useful image is to imagine the larynx being the same width as your body and moving downwards to connect to your sternum (which you can also picture as being the full width of your chest). This helps to make the connection a very physical one. The more you can connect your body to the singing the better.

As I mentioned before, it is the combination of the low, relaxed larynx working with your controlled breath that will give you a properly supported voice when you sing.

Note: ***Appoggiare La Voce*** *is an Italian expression meaning 'to lean on the voice' and is a term classical singers use when referring to singing with a low larynx.*

Relaxation Of The Larynx

Tension in the muscles of the larynx is a major contributor to tiredness and vocal problems. If you sing with a well-supported voice and you are producing the sound properly you should not experience any feeling of tension or strain in your larynx.

There is a great exercise to keep your laryngeal muscles relaxed whilst connecting the sound to the support which I call 'The Straw'. This is an amazingly effective speech therapy exercise often used in vocal rehab.

The Straw

This exercise is fantastic for not only relaxing your voice but also for warming it up. Clearly, it is very portable so you can do it when you're on the road or, as many of my clients do, in the morning when showering and getting ready to go out. You can use it throughout the day to manage your voice if it is getting tired. It is also very useful as a warm down after singing. It's such a simple but amazingly effective exercise – a potential tour saver!

As I have mentioned, the build up of muscle tension in the larynx is a problem for many voice users. This exercise can really help you relax the muscles. It is important though when doing this to make sure you are keeping your larynx relaxed and not forcing or straining anything.

Take a straw (you can use a regular drinking straw but my favourites are short 4mm frappe cocktail straws) and put it in your mouth, placing your lips gently around it. Now siren gently up and down on a sound – a bit like a mixture between a 'vv' and a 'ww'. You should feel the connection with your support. Gradually go higher, but make sure you don't feel any pressure around your throat. Keep it nice and relaxed. If that doesn't feel comfortable try starting higher and sliding downwards.

No air should be escaping through the nose and mouth. A good way to check this is to lightly pinch your nose closed; there should be no change in sound. Put your hand in front of the straw and check to feel the air pressure stays even as you go both higher and lower.

You can hold single notes, starting low and gradually going higher. It is imperative you don't force the sound. Now make the low notes louder and softer. You should feel the support engaging; the louder you go the more you should feel the support. This is a great exercise for strengthening the support and the connection to it (the transversus abdominis). It reinforces the muscle memory so the more you do it, the more your body gets used to producing the sound in this way. Remember the feeling is of drawing your tummy button in towards your spine.

You can then progress to singing simple tunes. Practice this daily for 5–10 minutes at a time.

Speech therapists sometimes give people with voice disorders thicker, soft silicone tubes (about 9.5mm in diameter) to do the same exercise but into water. This really helps the voice user to keep relaxed, and encourages the making of sound without effort from the muscles of the larynx.

Note: You can use a regular drinking straw into water if you are very careful to make sure your throat stays relaxed. Some people find it easier to connect with the support whilst doing it into water. I recommend only singing low, held notes if you're trying this. Don't go too high.

Always make sure your larynx is feeling relaxed and you are connected to the support when you do this exercise. As well as the other benefits mentioned, if done correctly this will help you develop your range.

Chapter 4
The Mouth And Jaw

The sound obviously has to come out of your mouth when you sing. However, the mouth's main function is not to act as a resonator. We use it primarily to shape the vowel sounds, and the lips, teeth and tongue all work together to articulate the consonants. If you have tension in any of these areas it can tie up your singing. Unhelpful tension in the jaw and tongue is particularly common.

The Jaw And Tongue

It is very important to keep a relaxed jaw and tongue when you sing as they are interconnected with your larynx. Any tension in these areas, therefore, will directly and adversely affect your singing.

Many singers find their jaws become very tight or tense and their tongues ache when they sing. These are probably the most common areas of tension amongst singers.

The tongue is connected to the larynx via the hyoid or tongue bone (see diagram page 35). It is a lot larger than you might think. Only the tip of it is visible in your mouth; most of it lies in your throat. When you sing, your tongue should lie flat in your mouth. Obviously, when you sing words, the tip has to come forward to help with the production of consonants such as *t*, *s* and *l*, but you should still keep your tongue as relaxed as possible at all times.

Some voice teachers make you do weird things with your tongue such as getting you to lift it high at the back – a 'technique' I was forced to suffer when I was younger. Avoid anything like this which feels too unnatural. Try not to press your tongue down at the back. Some people do this in an effort to keep a low larynx. If you do this you will invariably experience an ache around the base of your tongue. You should watch out for this.

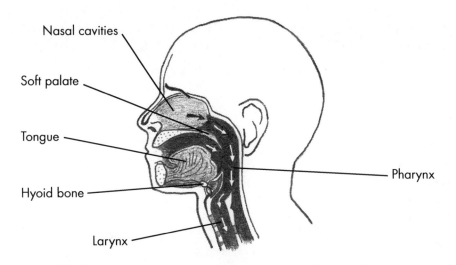

Nasal cavities

Soft palate

Tongue

Hyoid bone

Larynx

Pharynx

It is harder to keep your tongue relaxed when singing certain vowels. We are all different in terms of our mouth and throat shapes and sizes, and also, linguistically, regarding the accents we speak with. As a result of this we differ in the way we find certain vowels more difficult than others.

'Ee', for example, can be a tricky vowel sound for some people – it can make you pull your tongue up. 'Oo' can make you pull your tongue forward. 'Oh', 'awe' and 'ah' can also cause problems – some people will push down at the back of the tongue or tense the base of the tongue as they sing higher. In addition, many singers tense and almost lock their jaws on 'ah'.

You can think of the tongue being 'dumb' or 'stupid', just lying loosely in your mouth. Having some sort of image to help you let go of it is useful. You can visualise the base of your tongue being as wide as your shoulders and as low as your sternum.

Identifying where you have tension is the first step towards getting rid of it. With practice you can learn to let go of these tensions and free up your singing.

The Jaw

Most of us hold a huge amount of tension in our jaws. In the Far East there is a practice of jaw massage. Although uncommon in the West, after one of these sessions, apparently, you can feel amazing. However, I read somewhere the pain you encounter during the massage is close to that experienced during childbirth! (I don't think this is likely – probably written by a man.)

Joking apart, it is vital to have a loose, free jaw when you sing. It should hinge open smoothly and never come forward. Your chin should move down, or back and down slightly. If it comes forward you will put pressure on your larynx and tighten up your singing.

In The Groove

I love this! There is a groove you can feel through your cheeks between your upper and lower teeth, at the back. It feels like a small cavity on either side of your cheeks. Try to find it.

> *Place your index fingers in the grooves. Open and close your mouth. You can feel the movement of your jaw – how you can swing it forwards or back. Smile, as this lifts the soft palate and then sing allowing your jaw to release. It feels amazing singing whilst you do this. It gives you real 'freedom'. Sing a song with your fingers in this position. Note how much you want to bring your jaw forward and how easy it is to sing if you don't. The smile is an internal smile; it feels like you're lifting your soft palate up behind your cheek bones. If you don't have this lift the singing will feel squashed. Always remember to think down as you go higher, to keep your larynx low.*

I think of this as my 'get out of jail free card'. If you are having problems particularly with high notes in a song this will make singing the song feel much easier. It will help you to line up the singing and place it correctly.

Many singers tighten their jaws if they push their chest voice too high. As they drive the sound up, their chins and jaws tighten with it. You need to allow head resonance to 'mix' with the sound as you sing higher (see *Registers,* page 69).

Don't underestimate how bad a tight jaw can get. One person I used to teach had the most extreme jaw tension I have ever come across. She was doing a lot of singing on a course where the voice teachers were inexperienced and had very little knowledge of technique. She was a jaw-clencher, caused by an issue unrelated to singing. When she sang, her jaw frequently went into spasm and completely locked. It became so bad that her whole face swelled up and she could not move her mouth at all. She saw a medical specialist and was advised not to speak for a month! After her lay-off she had to start from scratch with her singing technique, but it was a real challenge for her.

Massaging your jaw can help you release tension. With your fingertips massage around your jaw line below your ears. Also, you can get in at the hinge of your jaw just below your cheekbones at the back.

The Mouth

Don't confuse singing with a visit to the dentist. When you are singing, you don't really need to 'open wide'. Again, this was one aspect of technique I was taught that introduced more tension into my singing than anything else.

As you sing higher you *do* need to open your mouth. If you are singing a song that uses a lot of high register and is a 'big' sing your mouth will need to be very open. If it is too wide, however, when you are singing low, the sound can be hard to control. You don't necessarily need to open your mouth as wide as you may think, particularly in the middle and lower registers of your voice. It is much easier to control the sound and keep it focused if you don't.

If your mouth is wide open, too much air can pour out and the sound can lose tone and focus. It makes it much more difficult to control the ends of phrases and it can often sound like the singing has 'collapsed', with the tone petering out.

A very open mouth position is widely used, particularly in classical music and 'open-throated' singing. While I am a fan of singing with a nice open space at the back of the throat, you don't need a wide-open mouth to achieve this (see *Open Throat*, page 62). Furthermore, if your mouth position is too wide in the lower registers, as you sing higher it becomes very difficult not to tense your jaw or bring it forward.

The Soft Palate

If you gently run a finger across the roof of your mouth, at the back you will feel a soft, squidgy bit. This is the soft palate. If you look in a mirror you will notice the uvula, which is the small pointy bit that hangs down from the soft palate. Some people confuse it with their tonsils – or even their vocal cords!

The soft palate needs to be lifted as you sing higher to allow the sound to move into the correct position (see *Registers*, page 69). If you don't lift it, the sound will stay too dark and will feel 'squashed' inside. The best thing to imagine is an 'inner smile' gradually increasing as you go higher. Some people think of it as a yawn. I was taught at one time to sing with a massive, cheesy grin on my face – even to practice singing whilst brushing my teeth. It might feel quite good for your jaw, but not only do you look a bit crazy when you sing, the sound loses all focus and becomes woolly.

The Pharynx

This is the name given to the area at the back of the throat. The back wall contains several muscles and these can alter its shape and size. The pharynx is a very important resonator (see diagram on page 35) and when you sing, this area should feel open and not squashed or restricted in any way. I often refer to the pharynx as being at the back of the mouth as it can be easier to picture. Some people get confused with the throat and think of the pharynx being too far down – almost at the back of the neck.

SECTION ONE SUMMARY

- It is not necessary to know anything about how your voice works in order to sing, but some knowledge of the physical processes involved will greatly help your understanding and development of technique.

- Although breathing is an automatic process you can exert some control over it. You can learn to use the muscles involved in breathing and in other parts of your body in ways that will maximize your ability to sing.

- To develop any control over your singing, you need to control the flow of air as you sing.

- The control of breath is known as **support**.

- Controlling the flow of breath with your **diaphragm** is the key to support.

- Correct support is achieved by combining control of the out-breath with a **low larynx**.

- Performing the exercises recommended in this section will help you to:

  a) get in touch with your breathing.

  b) become aware of the muscles involved in support.

  c) strengthen the support mechanism.

  d) maintain a low larynx when singing.

- A great deal of singing technique is learned through the use of mental control and imagery.

- Unwanted tensions in the jaw and tongue can adversely affect your singing.

- The **soft palate** needs to be 'lifted' as you sing higher.

SECTION TWO:
BODY TALK

In Section One we learned that the best way to produce and control the basic singing sound is by breathing properly, supporting the breath, and keeping a low larynx. We also saw how unwanted tension in the jaw and tongue can hinder our singing.

But singing involves your *whole* body. If you have unwanted tension in virtually *any* part of your body, it can adversely affect the way the sound is produced.

If you have a tense body, any tension will be transferred to your singing. Equally, if your body is relaxed, open and free, this will be strongly reflected in your voice.

In this section I will discuss the importance of keeping your body *open, wide and free*, and describe how to achieve this. We shall consider the particular challenges facing singers who also play instruments, since good body use for these people can sometimes be more difficult to achieve.

At the end of this section I shall briefly describe how such practices as Alexander Technique, Feldenkrais and Yoga can be particularly helpful to the singer, and I have included in this section some exercises of my own designed to free up your body.

Note: In Section Three we consider the important concept of *resonance* – the way we use key areas in our body to *resonate* the sound in order to amplify and add colour to it.

Chapter 5
Open, Wide And Free

The importance of having a free body when singing cannot be overemphasised. As we have seen, tension, not only in the jaw and tongue, but also in other areas of your body, can detrimentally affect your singing quite significantly.

In terms of body use I have a mantra for all singers:

WHEN YOU SING YOU SHOULD BE **OPEN**, **WIDE** AND **FREE**.

Let me explain. What happens when we sing with a free body? Have you noticed, for example, how well you can sing in the bath or shower? It's partly that the acoustics in a bathroom are often helpful, of course, but our bodies are also invariably very relaxed and tension-free at these times. Our voices flow through our bodies freely and fill the room with sound. It's never the same if you think someone is listening because you immediately tense up!

The ways in which singers perform live vary considerably. Some singers are quite static when they perform; others throw themselves around dramatically. A very physical performance can be exciting, but there is, however, a risk of the singing being compromised. The opposite, though, is usually the case. Many singers achieve an open and free body this way, which in turn liberates their voices.

Equally, if you are a person who naturally gestures and moves when they sing, forcing yourself to keep still can seriously affect the freedom of your singing. It shuts down the physical connection you have with your voice and stops the flow of energy.

Let's see how we can open up our bodies in a helpful way, and what we can do to avoid unwanted tension.

Standing

Ideally, when you are singing, you should stand with your feet the width of your hips apart. Your head should be balanced, shoulders relaxed, and your chest open but not pushed forward. Make sure you are not tensing your legs or your bottom. Your body should feel relaxed, balanced and open. Try, as much as possible, to maintain this posture when singing.

Even when you are not standing still, try to keep these principles of good body use in mind. The more demanding the singing, the more attention you should pay to the way you use your body.

Ideally, you should experience a 'free' body not only when standing but also when sitting and singing, playing an instrument, or moving around the stage.

The Head

You will have seen many singers pulling their heads back in an apparent attempt to hit the high notes or pushing their heads down to reach the low notes. Psychologically you may feel it helps you as people generally associate singing high with reaching, and singing low with pushing down. Throwing your head around in this way may look dramatic, but it is not at all helpful vocally.

Don't pull your head back or push it down as this will not only put pressure on your larynx, it will also affect the connection with your breath. If you consider what's happening physically when you do this, the air is prevented from having a totally free passage to your vocal cords. Keep the back of your neck 'long' at all times. Incidentally, also be careful when singing with a mic stand – ensure the stand is neither too high or low, as you want to be able to maintain a balanced head when singing with a mic.

Put one hand on the back of your neck. Pull your head back. You can feel it squashing the back of your neck. As you do this you will also collapse forward across your chest and shoulders. Then place a hand gently on your throat. Now pull your head back and feel the tension in your neck and throat.

Body Tension

Legs And Bottom

Don't tense these. If you do, it will be hard to keep your breath relaxed and low. It mays also make you tense your back and shoulders.

Shoulders

Keep these relaxed. Don't hold them up by your ears, keep them opening back and down into your shoulder blades. Don't push them forward. If you tense your shoulders it will inhibit the free flow of your breath and tighten up your singing.

Arms

Relax your arms and hands. If you clench your fists you automatically clench other parts of your body. Tense arms and fists, for example, restrict the freedom of your breathing.

Occupational Hazards

It is not only what you are doing when you are singing that can cause you problems. How you use yourself in everyday life, particularly at work, can throw your body out of line. Take, for example, being slumped over a keyboard or staring at a computer screen for much of the day. It really is very difficult in these situations not to 'collapse' your body and to stay open across your chest.

We can build up so many tensions without even being aware of them and then it becomes very difficult to leave these tensions behind when we start singing. I know there are a lot of things to think about all at the same time, but once you adopt certain habits good body use will soon become second nature.

Here is a series of exercises that will make you more aware of your body and what you are doing with it when you sing. If you practice these you will gain more freedom in your body and therefore in your singing.

Exercises To Free Up Your Body

The position for this exercise is the same for three-stage breathing (see page 18). In this exercise you are not only concentrating on the breath but on 'letting go' of tension in your body.

Lie on the floor on your back with your head resting on two average-sized paperbacks (this supports your head and ensures you're not scrunching up the back of your neck). Bend your knees, keeping your feet flat on the floor, and rest your hands on your tummy. Breathe in and out through your nose slowly and deeply.

Concentrate on your back spreading into the floor; feel your ribcage and shoulders opening out onto the floor. Think about your chest getting wider and your body longer. Try to let go of your neck (remember the weight of your head is being supported by the books not by the muscles normally employed).

The following exercise gives your back a lovely twist, and opens you out across your chest.

Lie on the floor as above. You may want to try this without the books, it's up to you — whatever feels best for your neck. Stretch your arms out to the sides of your body, palms facing upwards. Keeping your knees together and feet on the floor, breathe out and rotate your knees over to one side. You may find it feels good to turn your head the opposite way. Stay here for a few minutes (if it doesn't feel comfortable, come up, breathing slowly). When you have had enough, breathe in and bring your knees back to the middle. Breathe out and rotate your knees over to the other side, turning your head the opposite way. Make sure your shoulders are in contact with the floor — if not you should stretch your legs out more or lower your arms slightly.

If it feels very easy, you can repeat the twist starting with your knees over your chest and feet off the floor. Be careful not to put any strain on your back. If you feel it pulling, put your feet back on the floor.

Exercises While You Sing

When I introduce these exercises to people they often ask whether I have a hidden camera in the room for blackmail purposes – how soon will it be before clips appear on YouTube? The exercises are fun and admittedly a bit strange initially, but trust me they all serve a serious purpose so please try them!

While you sing, hold a plant pot or large glass on your head. Don't worry, you haven't got to balance the object. Hold it with both hands, keeping your chest open and elbows pointing out to the walls. Not only will you feel that it's easier to breathe, but your head will be balanced and your body open and stretched. It is all well and good to tell people not to pull back their heads when they sing, but singers who do have often developed a very strong habit which is difficult to break. This exercise reinforces the feeling of singing with a well-balanced head.

Singing whilst balancing a bean bag on your head also works well to keep your head balanced. As soon as you move your head back the bean bag will fall on the floor.

This next exercise gives you a great stretch and opens you up across your chest and shoulders as you sing.

Stand up straight and take the thumb of your right hand over your right shoulder as if you were hitchhiking. Next, stretch the arm out as far as it will go to the side, pointing your fingers. Put these two things together in one smooth sequence. Hold the stretch. Take your arm down and repeat on the other side.

If you only stretch your arm out without the 'hitching' movement, it is not as effective. This is because the 'hitching' rotates your shoulder outwards and opens out your chest more.

Now sing and do the exercise. Every time you take a breath, swap sides. It takes a bit of practice to co-ordinate everything, but it's well worth it.

Another simple thing to try is to let your arms hang loosely by your sides, and then swing them backwards and forwards as you sing. This will liberate your singing as it helps to loosen you up.

Walking rhythmically (and marching) as you sing is very helpful. Singers often find that they build up tension if they are standing still and concentrating. Swinging your arms while walking is even better for freeing you up.

> *Singing whilst 'scrubbing' your back is another great thing to try. Imagine you are scrubbing your back from above with a long brush. Have a good 'brush' one side then change arms. This action helps to open you up across your chest.*

Similarly, whilst singing, rub your back with a towel. Hold it with both hands and move it up and down diagonally across your back. When you have had enough change sides. Again, this opens you up across your chest.

> *Stand with your arms at shoulder height stretched out to the side with one palm of your hand facing upwards towards the ceiling and the other palm facing the floor. Now reverse this by turning the hand facing upwards down to the floor and the hand facing down upwards to the ceiling. As you do this lean to one side and then the other in a sort of gentle 'lunging' movement. I call this my 'fencing' exercise. It is wonderful for opening up your sternum (breastbone), an area in which we hold onto all sorts of 'stuff'. Most singers experience a feeling of tremendous freedom and release in their singing when doing this and it is an absolute favourite of many of my clients. It is based on a Feldenkrais exercise (see page 53).*

Chapter 6
Singing With An Instrument

There are many examples of great singers who also play an instrument. In fact, clearly, in many instances their playing complements and enhances their singing performance.

There are, however, some problems to overcome when singing and playing simultaneously. It is easy to find yourself falling into bad ways of using your body – in other words, doing those things that prevent you from maintaining a body that is open, wide and free.

The Pianist

When singing and playing, stay open across your chest. Keep your shoulders relaxed; try not to lift them. Make sure your elbows aren't stuck to your sides. Don't hunch over the piano as this will restrict the space for your breath and make it hard to sing long phrases or have any volume.

Keep your head balanced; if you pull it back you will lift your chin and shorten the back of your neck. This will put pressure on your larynx and make it difficult to connect your voice to the breath.

Avoid pulling your head around – you will lose stability in the sound and connection with the breath. We have all seen famous artists break these rules, but trust me, it's better for your singing if you don't!

If you are using a mic at the piano, be careful about its position. Place your mic so you don't have to lean forward or pull your head too far up or down to reach it. If the mic position is awkward you may find it difficult to keep your head balanced and stay open across your chest and shoulders. As a result, the singing may feel restricted. Be careful to keep the length in the back of your neck.

Similarly, you need to be careful about your mic position when standing and playing keyboards.

The Guitarist

The singer-guitarist also needs to be aware of how poor body use or habits can affect their singing.

Some guitarists I have worked with experience problems with their breathing and breath control. Holding the guitar awkwardly (from a singer's point of view) can cause specific problems: it can throw your body off balance and may result in you developing strange things to compensate.

People adopt all kinds of unhelpful physical habits and mannerisms when they sing: slumped bodies, stiff shoulders, tense jaws and chins etc. The most extreme case I have come across involved someone who would jolt his right side up, and then down, by about 5cm (2") every time he breathed in. The main problem stemmed from the way he held his guitar. He always played with it slung extraordinarily low on the right side and had done so for about ten years. The only possible way he could get enough breath (because his rib cage and lungs were squashed) was by making an extreme and exaggerated physical movement. By making him aware of this, and by strapping his guitar a bit higher, his singing greatly improved.

Ideally, when you sing, you should stand as I've already described (see page 42). Many guitarists find their guitars actually help them with their support. If you have your guitar resting against your tummy you can breathe 'into' it, and use it as an anchor to support your singing through a song.

Guitarists may want to try this version of the diaphragmatic breathing exercise already described.

> *Put your hands on your tummy, just below your tummy button. Breathe in slowly through your nose. Feel your tummy moving out. Breathe out in short bursts on a 'vv' sound, feeling your tummy muscles 'springing' in. Remember, you draw your tummy button in towards your spine. Now do the same whilst holding your guitar. Breathe into it. Now play and sing, trying to keep your breath in this low place.*

Guitarist's Chin is a name I've coined for a very common problem amongst guitarists. I have a theory this strange condition develops as a result of songwriting and playing in the bedroom late at night! Budding singer-songwriters often find themselves sitting on the edge of their beds strumming away, trying to keep the noise down. Hunched over their guitars, searching for inspiration, they pull their heads back. In a desperate attempt to be as quiet as possible, they either hum or mumble the words with their lips quite closed. Their chins lock and their jaws get very tight, particularly as they sing higher.

In addition, the sound can become very nasal in quality. *Guitarist's Chin*, then, combines several aspects of bad body usage that will inevitably restrict your ability to sing well.

To be quite serious, it is easy to fall into bad habits and I know many guitarists for whom this is a real problem. Jaw tension is pretty widespread amongst singers as I have mentioned before, and *Guitarist's Chin* is a definite contributor. People prone to *Guitarist's Chin* should try the following:

> *Try to keep your lips, not your jaw, forward as you sing in your lower or middle register (as you go higher you will have to open your mouth and the back of your throat more). Practice singing, without playing, with your fingers in 'the groove' (see page 36). This will help to ease any tension and prevent tightening in your jaw. Try to stay open across your chest and shoulders as you play – whether you are sitting or standing.*

You should be at one with your instrument when singing and playing. There are other things you can do to feel freer in your body. For example, aim to learn your guitar parts thoroughly before you accompany yourself. Your playing should be as automatic or 'second nature' as possible so that you are free to think about your singing. If you are playing rhythm guitar, get the rhythm as solid as possible before adding the vocals.

KEY POINT

If you play guitar or keyboards as you sing, avoid hunching or 'collapsing' over your instrument and be careful to position your mic in such a way as to keep your body as 'open' as possible.

Combining singing and guitar-playing well is quite a skill. For pure genius at it you need look no further than the great Jimi Hendrix. What you are trying to achieve is a state where you feel that you, your guitar playing and your singing are at one. When you watch footage of Hendrix you just know that was the way he felt when he was in the groove. The way he got locked into every aspect of his performance is mesmerising, totally satisfying and thrilling. He was particularly good at those little guitar fills between vocal lines that help to create an unusually intimate relationship between guitar and voice.

To get on top of playing and singing, either with piano or guitar, my advice is to practice both separately until each one is secure, before finally putting them together.

Chapter 7
Helpful Practices

The Alexander Technique

As we have seen, it is essential you develop an awareness of how you should be using your body when you sing. Something that has helped me achieve this is the Alexander Technique.

Many people with back problems, and other chronic pain sufferers, have found Alexander Technique very helpful.

But you don't have to be experiencing obvious problems to benefit from the technique. In fact, it is an assumption amongst Alexander practitioners that most people are 'misusing' their bodies to some extent as a result of learned bad habits – a near-inevitable consequence of modern-day living.

It is difficult to summarise what the technique really is, and in fact if you asked a dozen Alexander teachers they would all give you a slightly different answer. For most it represents an entire way of life. Proponents of the technique regard it as an essential guide to how everyone should use their bodies (and minds) healthily in every aspect of their life.

Alexander himself said of the technique:

'My technique is based on inhibition. The inhibition of undesirable responses to stimuli, and hence it is primarily a technique for the development of the control of the human reaction.'

The technique is about establishing patterns of good body use, whilst 'inhibiting' or trying to let go of, old bad habits (of body misuse). Most people will learn the technique literally in a 'hands-on' way. The teacher uses their hands to 're-coordinate' the pupil. A lot of work is done with the pupil lying on a table, with the teacher laying their hands on. Sometimes the teacher will work with you sitting in a chair or standing (or moving between the two).

The teacher works gently, focusing on different areas of your body. They may take one arm at a time and then each leg, gently guiding them and encouraging your body to release muscle tensions. They also do a lot of work opening you up across your chest and shoulders. My absolute favourite is having my head 'taken'. You are encouraged to let go of your neck with the teacher taking the full weight of your head in their hands.

As the teacher 're-coordinates' your body, they give you instructions on how to direct your new body use. Much of the emphasis is on 'lengthening and widening' your body and 'freeing' your neck.

It can take a long time to learn the technique and for you to be able to use it without thinking in daily life. Most people don't have the inclination to pursue it fully; it is the 'hands-on' work done by the teacher they enjoy the most and from which they gain the most benefit.

I had Alexander lessons for several years and use its main principles in my teaching every day. It has taught me to be 'in tune' with my body as I sing, and I have become more aware of myself physically and mentally when I use my voice. I have developed an understanding of what it feels like to sing without excess tension anywhere. It has helped me to sing with an open and relaxed body and a balanced head. Above all, I have learned to be *open*, *wide* and *free*.

There is nothing quite like the feeling you get from having an Alexander lesson. It opens up parts you didn't know existed. In the right hands it makes you feel absolutely wonderful – having your head 'taken' and your neck lengthened: pure bliss!

A Brief History Of The Alexander Technique

Frederick Matthias Alexander was born in Australia in 1869. In his early twenties he became an actor, specialising in one-man Shakespearean recitals. He soon encountered voice problems. His voice became hoarse, and eventually he lost it altogether during a performance. Doctors were unable to help him and simply prescribed rest. His voice did recover after a few weeks, but as soon as he went on stage again the same thing happened. He therefore deduced the root cause of the problem lay in what he was doing as he performed.

He then spent several years examining himself in minute detail in front of mirrors to try to identify what it was that had caused his voice loss. He observed, amongst other things, that when reciting he would:

Pull his head back onto his spine;
Put pressure on his larynx;
Gasp air into his mouth.

In time he realised he also did these things during normal speech but it was more exaggerated during performance. Gradually, he developed a way of 'inhibiting' these habits and using his body in a more efficient way, enabling him to rebuild his voice completely. He started to teach other people his methods and his approach became known as Alexander Technique.

Feldenkrais

Another practice that is about good, efficient body use is Feldenkrais, which can be described as a self-discovery process using movement. Individuals are taken through movement sequences e.g. sitting, standing, walking, breathing, etc. to 'discover' a better way to perform these functions. By aiming to re-program the functioning of our nervous system it helps us overcome many of the physical problems we may have developed over the years. There are similarities with Alexander Technique in as much as the teacher will sometimes work in a 'hands on' way.

Since studying Feldenkrais I have become so much more aware of my body and how all the various parts are inter-connected. It has completely changed my posture, making me much more open across my chest and shoulders. This has hugely benefited both my singing and piano playing. It has really transformed my breathing and I have a much more developed sense of how I use my body when I sing. Also as far as my overall well-being is concerned, I have markedly less tension in my neck and shoulders and all my joints move much more freely.

The Feldenkrais method can really help to improve movement and enhance how your body functions. It is great for relief of muscle tension and muscular pain, particularly for people with back problems. It can help you improve your performance in music, dance, sport and drama as well as giving you greater freedom in everyday activities.

A Brief History Of The Feldenkrais Method

Moshe Feldenkrais (1904–1984), the method's originator, was a distinguished engineer and physicist, as well as a respected Judo instructor. When he was young he sustained a terrible knee injury and by middle age he was threatened with severe disability. He was told he needed surgery but there was a high chance he wouldn't be able to walk again. He refused the surgery and instead applied his extensive knowledge of anatomy, physiology, psychology, engineering and martial arts, to the healing of his own knee. At the heart of his painstaking investigation into how he organised himself to move, was his precise attention to the details of function. He studied closely how one sits, stands, bends to the side, rotates etc. and eventually managed to heal himself. It was this attention to function that lead Feldenkrais to develop his method.

Yoga

Yoga is another practice which has helped me develop an awareness of how I use my body and also, very importantly, my breath.

It goes without saying there are many health benefits to be derived from practicing yoga, but in this book I want to consider specifically how yoga can help to improve your singing.

Yoga is said to describe the 'union of the physical body with the mind and spirit' and therefore the learning of meditation techniques is invariably an important element. There are many different types of yoga, of course. I practice Hatha Yoga, which has a real emphasis on breath and getting in touch with your breathing. Hatha Yoga helps you develop an awareness of how to relax and deepen your breath, which is so important when singing.

It is also wonderful for stretching and opening up your body, as well as relieving tension and increasing your energy levels. If you practice yoga, you will develop an awareness of how you are using your body not only when you sing but in everyday life.

I use yoga breathing exercises to help performers relax fully before they go on stage. The exercises work brilliantly. If you are feeling nervous or anxious in any situation – you may have an audition, job interview, or have to give a presentation, for example – the exercises will calm your breath and stop you going into 'panic' breathing. I described the three-stage breathing exercise earlier – give it a try. It is a very powerful tool.

The meditation side of yoga can also help you with positive visualisation for performance, which is something I shall be dealing with later.

General Exercise

Singing involves the whole body and it will therefore help if your general fitness is good. Running and swimming are great – in fact anything aerobic.

In one old, extremely quaint book on choral singing I read, the author recommends 'romping and mushroom-picking' for loosening up the hips. Well, I don't think many of us are averse to a bit of 'romping', but us city-dwellers are rather starved of opportunities when it comes to mushroom picking.

On a serious note, be careful when working out in the gym, especially if you are lifting weights or doing sit-ups. Try to avoid putting pressure on your larynx – when doing exercises constantly monitor yourself for any signs of strain here. Always get a professional coach to help you plan a suitable programme and to check you are doing the exercises properly. Remember, however, that such coaches are not voice experts, so you must still be on your guard. It doesn't surprise me that many people develop very 'tight' voices during and after working out, and this can eventually lead to voice problems.

SECTION TWO SUMMARY

- How you use the whole of your body has an effect on your singing. In particular, unwanted tension in certain areas can adversely affect it.

- As you sing, try to maintain a good standing posture: head balanced, shoulders relaxed, chest open, with no tensing of the legs or bottom.

- Do not pull your head back when reaching for high notes, or push down when going for low notes.

- The exercises in this section will help you to become more aware of how you should use your body.

- Singers who accompany themselves on an instrument face particular physical challenges. There are specific things that these people can do to maintain good body use.

- Alexander Technique, Feldenkrais and Yoga are all highly recommended practices for singers.

- Most general exercise, and particularly aerobic exercise, will benefit the singer, although care must be taken in the gym to avoid doing anything that puts strain on the larynx.

SECTION THREE:
GET SINGING

We have already seen how the raw sound is produced and that what you do with your body can adversely or positively affect it. Now I'm going to deal with the 'ins and outs' of singing – in other words, once you have made the sound, where you send it and what you do with it.

If you take on board the information in this section and put into practice what you learn, you will begin to experience huge improvements in your singing.

Firstly I will talk about *resonance* – how and why you 'resonate' the sound. I will then go on to discuss different *registers* and *voice types*, as well as the use of *falsetto* and *vibrato*.

We'll then move on to examine the way you sing words and how this has a huge impact on the sound you make. You will learn about *singing on the vowel* – an aspect of technique that has transformed many people's singing overnight.

Then I shall deal with the musical side of things. What is it, in fact, that distinguishes the great singers from the merely good ones? Included in this section is a close look at what is meant by *style* and *phrasing*.

Improvisation is something many singers find difficult and worry about. I suggest a simple approach to get you started. *What key do I sing in?* is a question I am often asked. I shall explain why the question doesn't actually make sense. Other relevant topics such as *pitch, out of tune singing, perfect pitch* and *relative pitch* are also discussed.

Finally, I shall talk about the importance of *warm-up exercises* and give you some to try.

If you have followed the basic instruction up to this point, you should now prepare yourself for some very exciting, accelerated learning.

Chapter 8
Resonance

What Is Resonance?

Resonance refers to the way the bones of the head and upper chest and the air cavities of the pharynx, mouth and nasal passages amplify and change the quality of the basic vocal sound you produce.

In order to appreciate the importance of resonance let's start by considering the following celebrated singers: Frank Sinatra, Billie Holiday, Ella Fitzgerald, Pavarotti, Sting, Aretha Franklin, Freddie Mercury, Stevie Wonder and Amy Winehouse. The first thing you can say about all of them is that each has an instantly recognizable voice.

So what lies behind the individual quality of their voices? Certainly they all have a strong *stylistic* identity, being each in their own way masters of style and phrasing (which we shall come on to later). But there is more to it than this. The key to each artist's distinctive 'voice' has its origins in the individual way they produce and *resonate* the sound.

Of course, every singer has a unique voice and this is largely to do with the way we are made. Naturally, there are physical variations between us such as the width of the face, the shape of the cheekbones or jaw, the size of the vocal cords and, indeed, the various shapes and sizes of the 'resonating' cavities. All these elements combine to give each of us our own individual-sounding voice.

This does not mean, however, that you cannot do anything to improve or vary the resonance. You will discover that there are *choices* available to you regarding the type of sound you want to produce, and these are to do with where you decide to send the raw sound once you have made it. As we shall see, you can send the sound into different parts of your body in order to vary its resonance – each area producing a different quality.

Chest And Head Registers

In any discussion about resonance probably the most obvious place to start is the basic distinction between chest resonance and head resonance.

Put simply, when you sing a low note you should feel the vibration in your chest; when you sing higher notes you feel more of the vibrations in your head.

Chest resonance adds warmth to the sound; head resonance adds brightness. Again, you direct the sound through a process of mental control. In a well-balanced voice you can move from one to the other smoothly without any sudden gear changes. (See *Registers* page 69)

Resonance And Vowel Sounds

A good way to demonstrate the difference between chest and head registers is with reference to vowel sounds. As we shall see later (*Singing on the Vowel*, page 90), the singing sound only really happens on vowel sounds, and therefore an understanding of how you sing them is absolutely fundamental.

Different vowel sounds have different qualities and resonate in different places. Generally speaking, 'oo' and 'ee' vowels resonate in your head and around the front of your face. These are referred to as 'forward-placed' vowels. 'Ah', 'oh' and 'awe' resonate more in your chest and the back of your throat, and are 'open' sounds. However, by thinking or directing the sound into different places, you can change the basic sound of the vowel, making it darker, lighter or brighter, or more focused.

Furthermore, individual singers prefer certain vowel sounds to others because they find them easier to sing. Different vowel sounds can create tensions in some people: for example, many singers find they tighten their jaws when singing 'ah'; others find they tighten their tongues when singing 'ee'. With practice you can learn to overcome these difficulties.

The following exercise will help you to explore the different qualities of the vowels.

Sing part of a song purely on an 'oo' or 'ee' sound instead of singing the words. Now do the same with 'ah'. You will probably agree they feel quite different – perhaps one is easier than the other. The 'oo' and 'ee' resonate around the front of your face and head. 'Ah' generally resonates more in the back of your mouth and throat (and is often harder to control).

Sing the 'ee' again. First try it with your mouth in a wide 'grin'; then try it with your lips a little more closed as if you were to sing an 'oo'. You are likely to find the second position easier to control and the sound more focused. You should feel the 'buzz' of the singing around the front of your face.

This forward mouth position also helps you to relax the outer muscles of the larynx and stops you tightening your jaw and tongue. Practice singing songs on 'oo' or 'ee' with this mouth shape. Many people find it helps their singing to become smoother and more resonant.

Note: As you sing higher, you will need to open your mouth more. If you keep it closed, your singing will tighten up.

Singing on an 'ee' sound doesn't suit everyone, particularly those with bigger or heavier voices. Many singers experience tightness at the base of the tongue; in others it encourages their tongue to arch up and forward.

The 'ah' vowel is more connected to your chest voice and is darker and more open in quality. When you sing with open vowel sounds you have the potential to sing with a lot more power.

If you find you are tightening your jaw on the 'ah' sound, use 'the groove' (see page 36) to help you relax. Remember to smile inside as you go higher; this helps you lift your soft palate and allows the sound to move more into your head – otherwise it will become stuck in your chest.

Varying Resonance

Moving beyond the basic distinction between head and chest resonance, the important thing to learn is you can choose to 'direct' or 'place' the sound into different areas in order to vary or change its tone.

You can, for example, choose to resonate in a 'chesty', 'nasal', 'throaty' or 'heady' way. Take these singers: Rod Stewart, Thom Yorke, Neil Young and Tina Turner. You wouldn't have much trouble matching the singer to one of the above distinctive sounds. That is not to say these singers sing exclusively in this way, but that their individual sound features one of these characteristics strongly.

It is what you do with the sound once you have made it that is the key. Think of yourself as having access to a kind of 'sound palette'. You can, for example, make the sound darker by sending it into the back of your throat. You can make it brighter by sending it forward or 'smiling'; and a nasal tone speaks for itself. The choices you make regarding resonance will often be unconscious; furthermore, your sound is likely to be linked to the sort of music or the kinds of artists you like or have listened to a lot.

There is more to resonance than just a choice of style or tone. Understanding and using resonance is another piece of the jigsaw. What you do with the raw sound is very important. The sound you produce should not be 'dead' or lifeless; it should 'ring' or, in other words, it should 'resonate'. If you push it straight out of your mouth, you instantly lose control over it. You need to direct the sound into various different places in your head and body to add volume, warmth, richness, edginess etc. This is what gives someone's singing its individual character.

As a singer, *you are your instrument*. Guitarists have a sound box, or an amplifier and effects pedals, to produce and resonate their clean or raw sound. Singers don't have that luxury. Obviously, if you sing with a mic, your voice is amplified. You can add some effects such as reverb, but this won't do much to enrich your tone or give you real sustain. We have seen that if your body is free, the sound you produce will be free. Let's look in more detail at how to do this.

There are various places you can send the sound for different effect: the back of your mouth, your head, the front of your face, or a combination of these.

The power of the mind is so important when singing. I use a great deal of mental imagery when placing the sound. Simply by 'thinking' of the sound resonating in a particular place you will find it will miraculously go there.

Thinking Big

When singing, I always think on a large scale. For example, I find it helpful to imagine a 'singing tube' that starts at head-level and reaches down into my whole body. I imagine it is the size of a huge barrel, or even a concert hall!

As I sing, I feel my entire body filling or resonating with sound. I always have this feeling anchored in my mind, and it helps to keep me 'open'.

Similarly, if I am thinking of the back of my mouth or throat, my mental image takes on the proportions of an open cavern. If you think 'big' in this way, it certainly has a more powerful effect.

Open Throat

One of the chief resonating spaces is the large area at the back of the mouth or throat known as the pharynx. As you sing higher you should visualise this opening up. It is essential to develop an awareness of this space if you are going to a have real 'supported' power in your singing.

When you sing using this space you are 'singing with an open throat'. You need to keep this space open as you sing higher to avoid tensing up your larynx. Think of an 'inner smile' – as if the corners of your soft palate are 'hooked up' behind your cheekbones.

Some people mistakenly think of the open throat too low down at larynx level. This can result in them pressing down with their tongues which, in turn, restricts their singing. It often makes more sense, therefore, for people to picture the back of their mouths.

Look at the cross-section of the head on page 35. This shows clearly how large the pharynx is. Imagine the space as if it is a wide cavern and send the sound here when you are singing. Raise your soft palate (see page 35) – feel it lifting – feel it lifting behind your upper back teeth. This will help you get the space open and 'high' enough.

Remember, as you sing higher, the natural tendency is to *reach* for the notes and raise your larynx. This results in your larynx tightening up. To be able to sing with as much freedom as possible, not only do you need to think of your larynx going down (see *Keeping A Low Larynx*, page 30), but you should combine this with keeping an open space in the back of your throat (remembering to support the sound, of course). This will give great security and depth to your singing.

The pharynx is not the only place to resonate the sound. If we only sent it there it would become too dark and 'plummy'. When I was young I was taught to sing with this 'position' for a number of years. My voice became incredibly strong but lost all its brightness. There is no doubt that working on resonating the sound in this area greatly strengthens your voice, but it is all a question of balance and personal choice.

It is important when singing higher to also allow the sound to move into your head. I imagine the sound coming up and over from the back of my head, over the top to the front. You may think of it in terms of riding on a roller coaster or a skipping rope coming forward over your head.

Forward Resonance

The area at the front of your face around your sinuses is an important place for resonating. Many opera singers refer to it as the 'mask'. The sinuses themselves don't provide a great amount of resonating space, and it is actually the bones in that area that resonate with the frequency. This is a very useful resonating space as you go higher.

Don't send the sound into your nose – you don't want it to become too nasal; place it around the sides of your nose and at the top of your cheeks.

Rest your hands on your face with your fingers lying across your cheek bones. Pick any mid-range note that feels comfortable and hum on an 'mmm' sound. Think of sending the sound here. You should feel a buzzing sensation . (If you feel it in your chest, try raising the pitch of the note.) Keep practicing as it will come eventually. You are now experiencing forward resonance.

Forward resonance can also be added by sending the sound into the area around your top lip. Put your mouth in an 'oo' shape and sing a mid-range note. Relax your tongue. The more you focus your top lip forward the more you will feel it buzzing or resonating. Keep your tongue relaxed. Move smoothly from an 'oo' to an 'ee' sound keeping your top lip as forward as possible. This is a very exaggerated position but well worth practicing to get the feel of it.

When you sing in the middle part of your voice with this forward mouth position it makes life much easier, but normally there is no need to exaggerate it as much. You will find you can sing longer phrases and don't lose as much air as when the position is more open. It also makes the sound nicely focused and is particularly good when singing anything in a conversational style.

Resonating around the front of the face is excellent for adding brightness to the sound. It is what I call 'forward resonance' or 'forward placing'.

Changing And Bending Vowels

As we have seen, you can change the quality of the sound you produce by resonating it in a different place. Sometimes you may want a whole phrase to sound bright, dark or chesty. You can achieve this by 'bending' the vowel sounds so that they resonate in the appropriate place: for a bright, 'ringy' sound, direct it into and around the front of your face and head; for a darker sound, direct it into the back of your mouth or throat.

You can also change the vowel quality by 'modifying' it. For example, pure 'oo' and 'ee' sounds primarily resonate in the head. Therefore, if you want to sing these vowels in your chest voice you would:

Change 'oo' to 'u' as in 'foot'

Change 'ee' to 'i' as in 'hit'.

This kind of vowel 'modification' really comes into its own when singing higher. As you sing up the scale, regardless of what vowel you are singing, you should always keep the space in the back of your throat open. You will need to change the shape of the vowels to 'anchor' them here. Let me explain:

If you sing a pure 'oo' or 'ee', with any volume on a high note your throat may well tighten. To avoid this, open your mouth, keeping the space in the back of your throat open, and direct the sound here. This will help you to keep the sound more supported.

The best example of vowel modification I can think of is in Stevie Wonder's *You And I*. Check out the final chorus. As his singing reaches a brilliant climax, he soars up to the word 'I' several times. Listen closely and you will hear him change the words 'you and I' to 'you and *awe*'. It is wonderful singing. You can hear the openness in his throat and the huge amount of power he has created. His singing here is almost 'operatic' in quality (he does add forward, brighter resonance, but it is predominantly 'open'). The way he 'bends' out of the final 'awe' back to 'I' is pure genius!

I have surprised a few singers by pointing out this particular example to them. It is the kind of thing the best singers do naturally and something your ear doesn't easily pick up. It is a demonstration of the way our brain fills in the gaps. Your brain expects a certain word and that's what you hear.

This technique is referred to as 'covering' by classical singers. The sound produced is 'darker' and the larynx position deeper.

Obviously, we can't all be as good as Stevie Wonder, but if you use this approach when singing high notes it can help you immensely.

Mimics And Clones

There are many 'soundalikes' and tribute bands who make a good living – some clearly better than others. The best mimics copy not only the mannerisms, phrasing and emotional content of the singing they are mimicking, but the resonance and voice quality. They have worked out the exact places where the original artist resonates the sound. It takes skill, patience and a great deal of practice to become very good.

I had the privilege and great pleasure of working with Jane Horrocks on the film *Little Voice*. Jane is an incredibly talented actor, singer and performer who is hugely committed and totally dedicated to her work. Many people still don't believe she sang all her own songs in that movie, but I can assure you she did – I was there!

Jane hears the particular resonance and quality in a voice and can instinctively copy it. But she doesn't just stop there. For *Little Voice* we spent many hours dissecting Judy Garland's 'sob', Billie Holiday's fragility and Marilyn Monroe's sensuality. Jane doesn't arrive at such brilliant performances by accident; she studies the singers in detail, listening to most of their repertoire, reading their biographies and watching them on video. She gets right inside the artist, and that is what makes her renditions so believable.

The scary thing about working with Jane is that you know that she is listening to you all the time, studying your every move and nuance of speech – often to use against you later!

Clearly, many of us are inspired by particular singers, and it is often this that gets us interested in singing in the first place.

Unfortunately, many young singers take this too far and become 'clones', all sounding like their favourite pop singer of the moment. Of course, you can learn a huge amount by studying another (good) singer's style and phrasing, and derive a great deal of pleasure from doing so. However, there is a danger that aspiring singers may pay attention primarily to the 'style' of a favourite singer at the expense of achieving any real 'substance' or technique to their singing.

The Stage School Sound

Some years ago now I was involved in helping develop a musical in its early stages. We needed to find a girl to play the part of a twelve-year old. We auditioned fifty girls between the ages of nine and fourteen from a well-known theatre school.

I was dismayed to discover that they all made a very similar 'produced' sound, with only one actually sounding like a girl. All the rest had the same pushed, 'showy' voices. Indeed, many of the girls sang very out of tune on the higher notes in an attempt to 'belt' out the notes. They had been taught to sing in a certain way to produce a sound that would be desirable in the world of music theatre.

Apparently, no attempt had been made to enhance or develop the individual qualities of their voices. Some people find this type of 'stage' voice appealing, but it is not for me I'm afraid. Call me old-fashioned, but I think girls should sound like girls.

I strongly believe in taking people's natural voices and enhancing them with good technique, not 'forcing' them into a mould!

CHAPTER 8 SUMMARY

- Apart from factors relating to the physical differences between people, the key to a singer's individual voice quality lies in the way they produce and resonate the sound.

- A basic distinction is made between chest resonance and head resonance: broadly speaking, when you sing lower notes you will be resonating in your chest; when you sing higher notes you are resonating more in your head.

- You can choose to direct or place the raw sound into different areas in order to create a 'chesty', 'nasal', 'throaty' or 'heady' resonance.

- A chief resonating area is the **pharynx**. You should always be aware of this space when singing, even when singing with forward resonance.

- The more power you want, the more you will need to focus on resonating in the pharynx.

- It is important to sing with an 'open throat' as you sing higher, to avoid tensing up your larynx.

- Resonating in the area at the front of your face adds brightness to the sound and is known as 'forward resonance'.

- Different vowel sounds have different qualities and resonate in different places.

- By sending the sound into different resonating areas you can change the basic sound of a vowel.

- As you sing higher, modify the vowels.

- You can change the resonating qualities of whole phrases by 'bending' the vowel into different resonating places.

Chapter 9
Registers And Voice Types

There is some disagreement amongst singing teachers about registers. Some believe there is only one true register. I believe, however, there are clear physical differences when singing in the upper and lower parts, and that the voice should flow freely from one part to another.

There are two main registers, 'head' and 'chest', and it is learning to coordinate these and 'smooth out' the movement between them that is important.

These registers are also referred to as 'head voice' and 'chest voice'. When you are singing in a particular register, you will feel the sound vibrate in that area. So, if you are singing in chest voice you will feel the vibrations in your chest, and if you are singing in head voice you will feel the vibrations in your head.

Ideally, in a well-balanced voice there will be a smooth transition from one register to another. In order to make it smooth you need to combine the head and chest registers. This is referred to as the 'middle' voice or register, 'mixed' voice or *passagio*. It is not a true register in itself, but is a combination of the head and chest.

As you go higher, you should sing with more head voice in the sound, gradually letting go of the chest voice. It is vital for the maintenance of a healthy voice that you develop a good mixed register or sing well through the passagio. You can view it as a 'crossroads' that ensures you will move into head voice as you sing higher. In male voices this is a considerably smaller area than in female voices.

Many singers 'push' the chest register too high. Watch out for this: you can damage your voice as a result if you are not careful.

In a man's voice, the dominant register is chest. A woman, by contrast, naturally should sing with more head resonance.

What I find interesting is that most people's voices are similar in terms of where the registers actually change. In men's voices the change into head voice should start to happen around E above Middle C. This area is referred to as the passage area or *passagio* and here the singing should be a mixture of chest and head voices (this is the trickiest part for any singer to master). Pure head voice should then be established around F sharp.

Women's voices are slightly different. Interestingly, the change from pure chest to head is the same as for men – you should start to introduce head voice into the sound around E above Middle C. This is called middle or mixed register. As you sing up the scale you should gradually sing with less chest and more head voice. Be careful around G to A – it is easy to get stuck here; allow the sound to move up into your head. By C sharp, an octave (and a semitone) above Middle C, the resonance should be right in your head. Around F sharp it moves again, into a different higher, place in your head.

To help you get the sound into your head, use some mental imagery. Think of placing the sound in the front of your head. Imagine the top of a mountain sitting above your head; as you go higher the sound drops in from the top of the mountain into the front of your face behind the back of your eyes. I also imagine a thin, pointed column above my head and the higher I go the slimmer the column becomes.

When you sing in head voice your larynx naturally tilts forward. To allow this to happen freely, as I have already mentioned, thinking of the sound going 'up and over' like a roller coaster or skipping rope can really help.

Caution! This doesn't mean that your larynx is allowed to shoot up as you sing higher. You always need to keep the space at the back of your throat, raise your soft palate, and think of your larynx staying low. It is a bit confusing at first but it gets easier with practice.

Beyonce is a really good example of someone who sings with a very well produced mixed register. She has a great warmth but also brightness of tone which enables her voice clearly to cut right across any backing without straining. She has great technique and has so much line and power as well as great breath control.

When you sing it is entirely your choice as to how you use your voice. This information on registers should help you to sing with a well-balanced voice. However, you may choose to take your chest high or your head voice low, depending on the sound you want to produce. The most important thing is to understand what you are doing and be able to control it. If you learn to have control of your head voice it will give you many more options. It will also help to prevent the top of your voice becoming tight and strained.

Pushing The Top

Many rock and pop singers push their voices as they sing high, getting locked into their chest voices by constantly 'pushing' the top end. In other words, they are singing with too much force too high up. There is no doubt this can result in damage to your vocal cords. The more pressure you use, the more muscle tension builds up and the more you grip with the muscles around your throat area. This may result in your cords becoming swollen and, if you're not careful, the start of some major vocal problems.

People who sing like this often find it very hard to develop any head voice as their cords will not respond in the right way.

Head Voice

To avoid the problems outlined above, you need to know how to get into your head voice without a sudden jolt or change in volume. Incidentally, I am not talking about *falsetto* here – that's different and we'll come to it later.

Firstly, it is vital that you use the breath well. Keeping the breath well supported is the single most important factor in achieving even, sustained singing. Keep the breath low and relaxed in your body and feel free and open. If the breath is working well you are halfway there. Remember to think of drawing in your tummy button towards your spine as you sing.

Secondly, never 'reach' for the high notes or pull your head back. Always think 'down' as you go up; think of a see-saw: one end moves up as the other moves down.

In simple terms, when you are singing up the scale you need to allow your voice to move into your head. As I have said, I find it useful have an image in mind to help me achieve this: it could be a pathway starting at the front of my face, stretching up to the top of my head. As I sing higher, the sound gradually moves up this pathway. With experience you will be able to find this pathway without thinking. The singing will probably feel 'lighter' when you sing in your head voice, but don't regard this as a problem or a weakness.

It is generally easier for women to find their head voice than men. This is because women's voices resonate naturally more in the head than men's do. Men with low voices will not really have any head voice but those with high voices may have a lot, depending on just how high their voice goes.

Some people are resistant to working with head voice. Over the years, many singers I have worked with (both women and men) have been reluctant to use any head voice in their singing. They see it almost as an admission of failure not to 'push' their voice to its absolute limits or to virtual breaking point. When they do push their voices, they experience considerable discomfort, and often develop sore throats, voice loss etc. There is a misguided feeling in the rock and pop world that high singing is only ever going to be strong or 'authentic' if the chest voice is pushed to its limits. I strongly disagree.

> *Sirening is a good way to discover your head voice. Start low humming on an 'ng' sound. (Don't place it too far in your nose, it should be behind it, and be careful not to push down with the back of the tongue.) Slide right up and down your voice, as high and low as you like, making a sound resembling a siren. The idea is to get this smooth, with no gear changes. If there are some big 'jolts', don't worry, it will improve with practice. As you come down from the top it may help if you think of the sound being more forward.*

Many singers with whom I have worked have discovered, with time, the versatility and extra choices using the head voice gives them, and the different colours and textures it can incorporate into their singing. Some have learnt to build head voice into their singing to such a degree that their ranges have increased massively and their ease and enjoyment of performing has been transformed. Because they aren't repeatedly thrashing the tops of their voices they can sing much longer sets and their voices are far more resilient when touring.

Some singers find it provides them with more options for backing vocals – as an alternative, for example, to singing in falsetto for higher BV parts. In addition, they come to regard the use of head voice as good vocal practice which, by way of a bonus, helps them to preserve their voices.

Let me be clear, then. If your voice is going to function in a healthy way you must allow yourself to use some head voice in the sound as you sing higher. Without it you will find it difficult to sustain demanding singing schedules, and your voice inevitably will become strained and damaged.

Mixed Register

Women have a much larger mixed register than men, stretching from E above Middle C to the C above. The passagio area for men, as already mentioned, starts from the same place, E above Middle C, but only reaches as far as F (one tone up) with head voice starting on F sharp.

It is important for all singers who want to have balanced, well functioning voices to work on this place of transition. If you don't learn to sing with mixed register the sound can become too 'chested' and tight or very heady and 'light' as you go higher. Some singers don't mind this and indeed many sopranos never sing in their chest voice at all.

Many singers find it hard to know whether they're singing in mixed register or not. There is a sense of strength and freedom when you find the right place. To help you find it you can imagine a semi circle behind your head stretching from the back of your head down to the middle of your back. When you're singing low chest notes think about the sound being in the lower part of the semi circle, as you go higher you can 'swing' more into head voice or 'swing' both ways into both chest and head areas. To successfully sing in mixed register you need to combine both the chest and head registers. It is a very physical sensation and the feeling is very open in the back of your throat. It is almost impossible to achieve mixed register if the position isn't open enough.

You can also imagine the sound to be 3D, each note consisting of a bottom, middle and top. People who sing with too much chest in the sound often lack the 'top' third dimension or upper resonance and this can affect the pitching, with the singing sounding flat or slightly under the note. Equally a note with too much top can lack weight and depth as well as sometimes sounding a little sharp.

When singing in mixed register always approach the note from above, easing into it, starting with some head voice; if you start with too much chest in the sound it can easily become stuck.

The Break

Many singers, women particularly, talk about having a 'break' in their voices as they move from one register to another. This usually occurs around G to A above Middle C. There should, however, be **no** break, and the transition from one register to another should be smooth.

The Belt

'The Belt' is one of my least favourite 'techniques', but is something still promoted by many singing teachers. It is predominantly taught to music theatre singers but some pop singers adopt it as well. The technique involves pushing the chest voice as high as possible in order to create that 'music theatre' sound. Apart from anything else, personally I find the belted sound unattractive. I prefer the sound of someone singing with a well produced mixed register.

More seriously, as you can imagine from all I have just said, I regard this technique as fundamentally unhealthy for the voice as it puts far too much strain on it. Indeed, I have met many West End singers with severe voice problems relating to the way they have been encouraged to produce the sound.

There is a commonly held belief in some quarters that the sound will be too 'classical' if you sing with a well-produced voice. It doesn't have to be: your 'ear' will help you make the appropriate adjustments to the sound. If you learn to sing with a well-balanced voice you will be able to sing with a big voice in your upper range without straining. You will have a wider dynamic range and more control.

A friend of mine who has been in many West End shows now sings with what he calls a 'cheating belt'. He 'belted' for many years and suffered all sorts of voice problems, culminating in nodules. He knew he couldn't continue in the same way, so he taught himself to support his voice well; he employed 'forward placing' and connected this to his chest.

He now has a strong 'mixed' register and head voice. He describes the feeling as singing just behind the bridge of his nose combined with a very open space in the back of his throat. He can sing for hours like this with no pressure on his larynx and he produces a really powerful sound. He says that the difference in sound to his 'authentic' belt is hardly noticeable. It is interesting that he calls it a 'cheating belt' as he feels that he must be 'cheating' because his singing isn't hurting him!

Voice Types

Singers often ask what their voice type is. These are the main voice types, starting with the highest.

Women
Soprano
Mezzo Soprano
Contralto (Alto)

Men
Tenor
Baritone
Bass Baritone
Bass

These names have traditionally been used to describe the range of the human voice. However, it can be very difficult to classify a voice since so much of it is down to its weight and tone, and there are many different classifications within some voice types. This in turn can cause problems if the repertoire given to you is unsuitable and 'pushes' you in the wrong direction. Many mezzo-sopranos, for example, can sing as high as sopranos, but they just don't feel comfortable staying up high for as long.

Ranges

Soprano:

G below Middle C up to high C (and beyond). There are different types of soprano depending on the quality of sound and weight of voice: coloratura (high and florid); leggiero (light); lyric (warm tone, long flowing phrase); dramatic (heavy and dark); and spinto (a mixture of lyric and dramatic).

Mezzo-Soprano:

F below Middle C to 2nd B above Middle C. Voice type is weightier than soprano but lighter than contralto. These again can be divided into lyric, coloratura and dramatic.

Contralto:

D below Middle C to 2nd B flat above Middle C. This is the lowest female voice type. Characteristically the voice is weighty with a very warm tone. A true contralto is a very rare voice.

Countertenor:

This is the name for a male voice that is falsetto-dominated. The range extends from F below Middle C to the 2nd F above Middle C. Some

counatertenors vibrate their cords in the same way as normal singers, but the cords are stretched thinner.

Tenor:

C below Middle C to C above Middle C. This is the highest (non-falsetto) male voice type.

Baritone:

2nd G below Middle C to high G sharp. Weightier and richer than a tenor voice. There is classification within baritones also: light, lyric, dramatic, Verdi.

Bass Baritone:

Low F to high F sharp. The voice quality is lighter than a bass

Bass:

2nd F below Middle C to G above Middle C. The lowest male voice type.

Basso Profundo is the name given to a very deep bass whose range is 2nd C below Middle C to E above Middle C.

Many of us know where we feel happiest singing, whether it's high, low or mid-range and don't really need to know whether we are a soprano or tenor etc. Obviously, if you sing in a choir or sing classical music you will need to know. Also, if you sing musical theatre repertoire it is helpful to know your voice type.

Repertoire is often published in several editions – in different keys for a high or low voice, for example. For some people it is quite obvious what voice type they are. Those in the middle should take care. If, for example, having always thought of yourself as a soprano, you then join a choir and find you are straining, don't be afraid to admit it and ask to change to the alto part.

Tessitura is a term used to describe the range of the voice or piece of music. If a song is said to have a high tessitura, this means most of the notes of the song will lie quite high.

As I have already said, just because you can reach certain notes it doesn't necessarily mean you will be comfortable singing in this part of your voice all the time. If the tessitura of the material is consistently high or low it may be too much for you.

CHAPTER 9 SUMMARY

- There are two main registers: head and chest. It is important to coordinate the two and smooth out the movement from one to the other.

- To make this transition smooth, the head and chest registers combine. This is referred to as the 'middle' or 'mixed' register, or passagio.

- Although there are clear differences between male and female voices, from person to person, they are remarkably similar in terms of where the registers actually change.

- 'Pushing the top' or singing too high in chest voice as an alternative to moving into head voice is a common cause of voice strain amongst singers.

- It is very important, therefore, to know how to get into your head voice without a sudden jolt or change in volume.

- To allow your voice to move into head voice as you sing up the scale, it is useful to think of some mental imagery such as a pathway starting at the front of your face and stretching up to the top of your head, along which the sound climbs or moves.

Chapter 10
Falsetto

If you are not sure what falsetto sounds like, think of Justin Timberlake or the Bee Gees. Falsetto refers to the highest part of a man's voice – if you like, the 'choirboy' part. It is used a lot in pop and R&B singing to add a lightness to the tone.

Having a good falsetto definitely gives you more options at the top of your voice and more choices of texture. It can also help to preserve your voice as you can use it as an alternative to 'pushing the top'.

I like the sound of a well-produced falsetto, one that is smoothly linked to the rest of the voice. Achieving this can be technically tricky, but mastered with practice.

Some people dislike the use of falsetto and think of it as a complete 'cop-out', preferring the top of the voice to be 'pushed' and 'chested'. I strongly disagree.

The term 'falsetto' actually means 'false' voice. This would seem to suggest it is not a legitimate 'voice', but that is simply not the case. Falsetto is a definite, physically identifiable voice in its own right. Research shows that when singing in falsetto your vocal cords are lengthened, tense and thinned, and there is minimal vibration. The airflow creates a hole so that the cords don't come together fully.

From as early as the thirteenth or fourteenth century, it appears likely that male singers sang using falsetto. Certainly, throughout the history of Western music, men have tried to extend their range by blending head voice with falsetto. Classical male singers who sing mainly using falsetto are referred to as *countertenors*.

Castrato *is the name given to a male singer who was castrated before reaching puberty. This practice was followed mainly in Italy from the 16C to the early 1900s. It was an attempt to keep the purity of tone and high voice of the prepubescent singer, but it didn't always work! Only one castrato to my knowledge, Alessandro Moreschi, has ever been recorded and the sound is quite extraordinary.*

There is some disagreement over the terminology. Some teachers believe the head voice should be called falsetto. However, as I have tried to explain there is an obvious difference between the two.

When you sing in falsetto you will feel the sound occurs in a similar place to the head voice, but the tone and resonance produced are very different. Your falsetto may feel a bit 'disembodied', but this does not mean it has to be fragile or weak.

The falsetto of many rock and pop singers is very strong and can cut right across a band. Listen to Freddie Mercury or the flamboyant Justin Hawkins of *The Darkness*. To develop and strengthen your falsetto, apply the same principles of good technique you would to the rest of your voice.

Working With Falsetto

Men with naturally high voices tend to sing in head voice in the upper range, only moving to falsetto when it gets very high. Men with lower voices, who have a much more limited head voice (or none to speak of), start their falsetto lower. It is knowing just where to change that causes confusion for many singers.

Remember, it is vital if you wish to have a well-balanced voice that you develop a strong and secure head voice. You shouldn't bypass this and only sing in falsetto at the top.

You should be singing with some head voice around E flat above Middle C. For those with lower voices, you may not be able to take this any higher than F/F sharp. Don't worry if you can't, it is simply the limit of your range. If you want to sing higher then go into falsetto.

Women also have a falsetto, but very few use it. Again, many women incorrectly refer to their head voice as falsetto. In fact it is that peculiarly high place in which Mariah Carey, for example, does her 'squeaks'. The notes up here, above normal head voice, are sometimes called 'super-high' notes, or the 'whistle' register.

A strong falsetto can be a very useful tool. It can help you to extend melodies and vary textures. It is also extremely useful when singing backing vocals – particularly high, blended harmonies. Used as an alternative to high 'shouted' choruses when gigging, it has the advantage of helping you to protect your voice from undue strain.

It is fair to say that many singers do not use falsetto as well as they could. It is the change from full voice into falsetto and back that causes many singers problems. Often there will be a 'jolt' as the sound gets suddenly weaker or louder. You will frequently hear male singers attempting, but not really making, the change from chest to falsetto.

It can be hard to blend falsetto with the rest of your voice, and it can sound disconnected from your normal voice – resulting in a sudden loss of resonance and character. With practice you can make these changes more even.

Always keep the breath low in your body (around your lower abdomen). Don't tense your shoulders or snatch the breath into your chest. Keep your body relaxed. It is vital for the sound to be properly supported. Let the sound 'ring' around your head as if it is in a large bell tower.

In falsetto sing an 'oo' on E above Middle C. Hold the note. Think of placing it around the sides of the front of your nose. Repeat on 'ee' and then 'ah'. You'll probably find 'oo' the easiest as it has a very forward resonance. Try placing 'ee' and 'ah' in this same space; keeping a forward mouth may help.

> *'Ah' is generally trickier to sing in falsetto as it is a more open sound. Be careful to keep a flat tongue.*

Experiment by placing the sound forward as you go higher. Then sing it with a 'yawny' open throat. Play around with it and see what works for you.

Many singers find if they place the falsetto very forward, almost around the top of the nose and around the sinuses, it helps to free up the sound and make it more focused. Others prefer feeling it right up in their head with a very open throat to give them power.

It will probably be easier for you to go from chest voice to falsetto at first (rather than head voice to falsetto). Practice the change from low to high and then try it the other way round – going from high to low. Keep working the links and it will become more reliable. Think 'down' when you are moving in or out of falsetto – it will keep your larynx stable.

If you strain your voice, often the first part to 'go' is your falsetto. If the vocal cords become swollen through 'pushing' and misuse they cannot stretch and be free enough for the falsetto to happen.

A few years ago a high-profile recording artist, with whom I had been working, had got over-excited and thrashed his voice while singing at a couple of large arena gigs. I was called in to try and help out as his falsetto had totally disappeared.

Fortunately, with careful warming up (an issue we discuss later in do's and don'ts) he more or less got it back – although he couldn't sing anything on an 'ah' sound (it is an open sound and you use more air to produce it than you do with 'oo' and 'ee'). He had to cheat and change all his vowel sounds to 'ee's and 'oo's when singing in falsetto. He survived the gig, sensibly took a couple of days' rest and, I'm pleased to say, was fine thereafter.

Some people will never like falsetto singing, but I think it is a useful tool to have up your sleeve. Besides, wouldn't the world be poorer without, for example, *Good Vibrations* by The Beach Boys? There are some artists, such as the Bee Gees, who sang in it almost exclusively. However you choose to use falsetto, make sure you are doing so because you really want to, and not purely as a substitute for singing in head voice where your technique is lacking.

Choristers And Children's Voices

I defy anyone not to be moved by the pure voice of a good choirboy: there is such innocence and clarity in the sound. Surprisingly, however, the majority of choristers fail to develop into equally good singers when they are adults. Indeed, I have seen it reported that only 2% of choristers ever turn into fine adult singers, and I suspect the problem is partly due to voice misuse around the time their voices break.

Many boys are forced to sing too high for too long. On average, between the ages of 12 and 15 boys' voices undergo major physical changes. Sensible vocal practice would be to let them gradually sing lower parts and not put their voices under any kind of strain.

This is true of all children, whatever type of music they are performing. Many experts will not allow serious voice training to start until the age of 17 in girls and 18 to 19 in boys. Common sense needs to be applied here. I believe it is fine to continue singing, and, in fact, I teach many teenagers. It is good to get to grips with breath control and tone production, but if we want these young voices to last a lifetime, great care has to be taken to avoid any pushing or forcing of the voice at such a delicate stage of development.

The Breaking Voice

Many boys have a traumatic time when their voices break. Boys used to be advised to stop singing during this period, but modern thinking is that it is generally okay as long as care is taken. Some boys hardly notice their break is happening as it does so gradually. Others, however, experience something more sudden. Some voices take a lot longer than others to settle down. Many boys find it quite distressing to lose their higher range or 'bright' tone.

I try to encourage them to be patient and enjoy the different qualities of their 'new' voices. I never allow them to force their voices. I believe it is good for boys to sing during this period. If it is left too long, their voices can become very breathy, and they may find it hard to 'start up' again. Besides, for those who love singing, getting them to give up for any substantial length of time could be deeply upsetting.

CHAPTER 10 SUMMARY

- Falsetto refers to the highest part of a man's voice – not a 'false' voice, but another physically different voice in its own right.

- A strong falsetto should not be regarded as a 'cop-out', but as a very useful tool to have at your disposal.

- However, in order to have a well-balanced voice it is vital that you develop a secure head voice and do not bypass this in favour of a leap straight into falsetto.

- Many singers find the easiest place to sing in falsetto is forward, almost around the top of their nose and sinuses.

- Particular care should be taken with boys whose voices are breaking.

Chapter 11
Vibrato

Technically, vibrato is an oscillation in the pitch of the singing sound. It adds colour and warmth, but varies widely in nature and use. It occurs naturally, but an experienced singer will learn how to use vibrato the same way an artist applies colour to their canvas. Singers, like painters, make decisions about which 'colours' to use and when.

As I have said before, the most successful singers have distinctive voices. Whether or not you happen to like a particular voice, you can usually identify a well-known singer on first listening. Many things combine to make up a singer's individual tone or 'sound'. As we have seen, how and where a singer resonates the sound is one important element: they may favour a breathy, nasal, chesty or heady sound. Phrasing and accent are also distinguishing features, but a singer's individual use of vibrato is another major component.

Classical purists believe there is only one correct way of producing vibrato. In operatic singing, vibrato is used throughout. For most opera singers, the idea of turning vibrato 'on' and 'off' as a textual technique represents something artificial or 'manufactured'.

I had a singing teacher once who was a traditionalist and purist, and to be frank, a classical singing snob. He was absolutely appalled when he discovered I sang other styles of music. He believed there is only one *correct* way to produce the voice. I disagree. I believe any singer has the right to choose how they use their voice and how they produce the sound – and, for that matter, what kind of music they sing! I certainly don't take the view that any one singing genre is 'better', more valid or 'more important' than another. What concerns me is singing *well*, with good technique, regardless of singing style.

Some singers of early classical music choose to sing with no or very little vibrato, as they believe this was how it was originally done. There is endless debate amongst musical historians about whether this is true or not.

Rock and pop singers generally do not use a great deal of vibrato in their singing. Some do, but the sound is usually a lot more 'natural' than that of the classical singer. Rock and pop delivery or style is more 'conventional' and direct. There are, in effect, many different ways of using vibrato, and its use varies according to the particular genre of singing in question.

Most pop singers use vibrato sparingly. Soul and R&B singers use it more evenly. If you listen to a Stevie Wonder song you will probably be surprised by how much he mixes and matches – often using no vibrato, or just bringing it in at the last moment. He has a natural, 'smiley' vibrato and uses it very tastefully.

Show singers utilise a deliberate, exaggerated, often nasal vibrato. One of the most extreme examples is Ethel Merman, famous for, amongst others, her over-the-top version of *There's No Business Like Show Business*. A pronounced yet silky vibrato is very much part of the style of the great crooners such as Nat King Cole, Bing Crosby or Frank Sinatra.

Even within rock and pop its use varies widely. Singers such as Avril Lavigne and Hayley Williams (Paramore) don't use any vibrato to speak of. The vibratos of, say, Elvis Costello or David Bowie are particularly deliberate and distinctive. Adele uses vibrato very evenly and tastefully, and will alter its speed depending on the tempo of the song: in slow ballads it is gentle and lazy (a slow oscillation). Compare this to the incredibly fast vibrato of the Bee Gees. Many singers such as Amy Winehouse and Pharrell Williams use it just at the end of a phrase, or on sustained notes.

Guitarists And Vibrato

Several guitarists I know have studied vibrato in great detail. They have made a point of listening very closely to their favourite players' live performances and recordings in an attempt to work out the exact speed and quality of vibrato they particularly like. They will point out to you, for example, the difference between B.B. King's very fast, intense vibrato and the much slower vibrato typically employed by someone like Albert Collins.

The interesting thing about the use of vibrato and note bending in blues playing is that the original great blues guitarists and other instrumentalists were in effect trying to make their instruments resemble the human voice. The blues and blues-oriented music are all about communicating what you are feeling to your audience.

The choice of vibrato in the hands of the great guitar players like those mentioned above closely reflects the emotion being put across. An emotionally intense passage, perhaps expressing anger or frustration, requires a quicker, more intense vibrato; a more subtle passage dealing with feelings of love or sadness calls for a subtler, slower vibrato. Good singers also vary their vibrato in this way according to the emotional dynamics of the song they are singing.

Eric Clapton once said one of the most difficult things for any guitarist to accomplish is to produce their own natural-sounding vibrato; the point being that it takes time for the vibrato to become 'natural'– in a sense, for its use to become automatic. Ultimately, the best guitarists and the best singers reach a stage where they don't have to think about how or when to add it because it becomes a matter of 'feel'. Furthermore, many have created a vibrato in their playing or singing which is recognisably their own.

Incidentally, with reference to the way guitarists imitate the sound of the voice, it is interesting to note that this can be a two-way process. Listen to the singing of Anthony Keidis of the Red Hot Chili Peppers (who, as a matter of fact, uses vibrato very sparingly) and notice how his singing often echoes the string bending and other licks favoured by guitarists.

Working On Your Vibrato

If you have a well-supported voice, you will produce vibrato naturally. I would say, the freer the voice, the freer the vibrato. Moreover, you can use it in any way you choose. You can make it long or short; you can use it throughout a phrase or just at the end. In other words, control over vibrato gives you many more choices in your singing.

Many singers want to improve their vibrato, making it more consistent, even and controlled. However, for some singers, vibrato remains a bit of a mystery.

If you have no vibrato at all, I suspect your voice is too tight. You will probably be 'clamping' with the outer muscles of your larynx. A constant theme of mine is that your singing should be free and not 'held' anywhere. Always remember to breathe low and stay relaxed. You should continually check for any unwanted tension anywhere in your body, but especially in the throat, jaw and tongue areas. As I said before, if you are doing all the major things correctly, your vibrato should occur naturally. In this sense it serves as a good check on your technique.

Some singers produce an artificial, forced-sounding vibrato. It can sound okay but never free and relaxed.

Vibrato Exercises

The following exercises are designed to help you understand a bit more about your vibrato, how you make it happen, and how you can control it.

This exercise is in three parts:

> *1. Hold a single, midrange note. Try to use vibrato for the whole length of the note. Relax your body, jaw and tongue. Take a slow, deep breath. Think of drawing the sound in, not pushing it out, keeping it supported.*

Start off on the vowels 'oo', 'ee' and 'ah'. Stay relaxed; massage your jaw and chin with your hands as you are singing.

> *2. Hold a single note, but this time try bringing in the vibrato halfway through the note, Still draw in the sound.*
>
> *3. Repeat as above; just bring in the vibrato at the very end of the note.*

You can try making the vibrato by sending the sound into the front of your mouth, keeping your lips forward. 'Think' about the sound you want to make.

Try speeding it up and slowing it down. Try singing the whole note with vibrato or using it just at the end. Experiment. The confusing part is remembering to draw the sound into your body at the same time.

Now try varying the sound, sending it more into your nose and then into the back of your throat (this will sound a bit heavier and more 'operatic' – particularly if you are supporting well). Play around with it. If you find a sound you like, work with it. Don't worry if the vibrato is not happening initially – it will eventually.

When you have practiced on the vowels, move on to words. Start with single words, progressing to a few lines from a song. Try using vibrato throughout and then just at the end of a phrase or on the more sustained notes. It is up to you to choose how you use it.

Many singers find it feels a lot easier to sing using a mic with plenty of reverb applied. However, you should be able to add your own vibrato. I have known professional singers who rely far too heavily on using a mic, and in fact have no natural vibrato at all. This is very limiting because in a dry acoustic it will become almost impossible to sing, as your voice will become very tight. So start working on your vibrato and add yet another string to your bow.

CHAPTER 11 SUMMARY

- Vibrato is the vibrating of the singing sound and should arise naturally from a well-supported voice.

- Good singers will vary their vibrato according to the emotional requirements of a song.

- If you have no vibrato at all, you probably have too much tension or tightness around your larynx.

- Exercises given in this section will help you to produce vibrato and learn how to control it.

Chapter 12
Singing On The Vowel

When you sing, what is it exactly you sing? Words? Notes? It may sound strange, but how about vowels? Trust me. If you take on board what I have to say about 'singing on the vowel' you could be on the verge of a massive breakthrough. Whatever style of music you sing, understanding and applying what is meant by 'singing on the vowel' will make a huge difference to your singing.

I have talked a lot about resonance and the different qualities that the vowels have. I mentioned the specific difference, for example, between the brighter, more 'forward' EE vowel and the darker AH vowel. In fact, creating vowel sounds is absolutely fundamental to your singing.

You need to concentrate on the vowel in order to gain control of the sound, and enable you to sustain a musical line or, in other words, sing in a *legato* way. Let me explain further.

Try singing and holding a note on a selection of consonants: D, T, G, F, K, for example. It's impossible, right? True, you can make a humming sound on an 'm' and 'n', but that's about it. The actual singing sound only happens on the vowel sounds, which, in the above exercise, you can't help sliding into. If you want your singing to flow, therefore, it follows that you must spend as much time as possible singing the vowels and making the most of each vowel's resonance. This, of course, is why singing exercises are sung on vowel sounds (see page 119).

The main vowel sounds we use when singing are the following: **'ah'** as in heart, **'awe'** (yawn), **'oh'** (got), **'o'** (low), **'oo'** (moo), **'i'** (lid), **'ee'** (tree), **'uh'** (shut), and **'e'** (met). In any song, any note should only really be held on one of these sounds.

Take, for instance, the word 'love'. Sing it on any note and hold it for as long as you can. Think about the sound you make; it's mainly an 'ah' sound. Try it again. This time hold the 'ah' sound and count (in your head!) to 4, then bring in the 'v' consonant. Do it crisply; don't slide into it. Look in a mirror and sing it. Are you trying to close your lips before you actually get to the 'v'? Try not to anticipate the consonant – it stops you making the most of your resonance. If the consonant comes in too early it cuts the sound dead – there is just no way you can hold the note.

Okay, one word is not too bad, but let's move on to putting words together into a phrase or line. If you want to be able to sing a legato line you must be able to sing through every vowel. Firstly, say these words: "Will you still love me".

The sound pretty much stops between the words and is quite detached. Now try linking the consonant from the end of one word to the beginning of the next. This will keep the sound flowing right the way through. It should go something like this:

Wi – llyou – sti – lah – vme

Now sing it. Try it your usual way first and then my way. Sing right through each vowel. Feel the sound resonating. Try it first on just one note and then vary the pitch. You should begin to notice the difference. The more you apply this approach to your singing, the easier it gets, and the more sense it makes.

Once you are singing the vowels, remember to let them *cruise on the platform of supported air.*

KEY POINT

You can only really hold notes on vowel sounds which is why, for example, singing exercises are sung mainly on the vowels 'ah', 'oo', and 'ee'.

You will find some words trickier than others. Watch out for those ending in 'y' as they can make a *double* vowel sound (dipthong). Take 'cry' – the 'ah' is joined to the 'ee' as in cr–ah–ee.

Try staying on the 'ah' for as long as possible before bringing in the 'ee'. This will give you a rounder sound. If you move to the 'ee' too quickly the sound will be thinner. Sometimes you may want that effect, but it is good to be able to have the choice.

Of course, this is a general guide. The aim is to help you sustain a smooth (legato) line. This is naturally desirable in slower numbers, but interestingly you have to work even harder at it in the faster ones since the words come more quickly.

Clearly, all this does not mean that consonants are totally unimportant. On the contrary, they are equally as important but for different reasons. Without strong consonants the lyrics would lose their meaning and the song would lack energy.

Not only do you need consonants to make the words clear (what we refer to as 'good diction'), but they can also be used percussively. They are an essential part of what gives singing its groove and rhythm. It is the ability to 'spring off' consonants onto vowels that you need to work on. This will not only add more groove but ultimately much more line to your singing.

Learning to sing on the vowel is one of the most effective tools you can have to improve and enhance your singing. It will make the difference between your singing sounding like (for all you guitarists out there) a soaring Satriani solo or a string of sausages.

Naturally, a singer has to pay attention to the meaning of words in order to interpret and put across a song powerfully. But listen to the vowel element in the songs sung by any of the best and most convincing singers you know, and you will see how important it is.

When I first came across this method of singing the words, I wrote out all the songs I was learning in a similar way to my example above. After about three weeks it had become second nature. Try approaching songs in this way; it is well worth the effort.

Breathing Within A Song

I have already emphasised how crucial control of the breath is to singing. I want to reinforce something very important. When you sing, the breath should flow in a controlled yet relaxed way. Breathing in a relaxed way is the most important aspect of technique to master. If you get this right, pretty much everything else will follow.

If you have been practicing your breathing exercises you should already be feeling the benefits. Hopefully you now have a much greater awareness of your breath and are developing more control over it.

When it comes to singing a song, however, things start to get a bit more difficult. You may find you begin the song with plenty of air, but by the time you've finished the first verse or reached the chorus, the breath has become tight and, before you know it, your old habits have reared their ugly head.

Your focus should be on your out-breath. Note, the out-breath is the relaxing part of your breathing cycle.

It is a good idea to start any song by first breathing out slowly then letting the breath come in slowly in a relaxed way. This will set up the breathing correctly. If you snatch the breath in at the beginning you start off with it feeling tense, tight and high, and very probably it will stay like this for the whole song.

As soon as you get to the end of a phrase, let the breath in. Don't hang around in a state of limbo waiting to gasp in the air like a goldfish just before you sing. If you do snatch in the air, you will tighten across your chest and shoulders, and your breath will be too shallow. Also, if you gasp like this it is easy to 'over-stuff' yourself with air. Your body will become tense, your sound breathy, and you will only be able to sing short phrases. In addition you will probably get head rushes.

Breathing in as soon as you have used up the air makes you take in the air efficiently. Try it. Put your hands low down on your tummy, breathe out, let the breath in and sing a phrase. As you finish, your tummy should be 'in'. You should be able to feel some muscle tension here and the connection with the support. If you support the ends of phrases properly, this will happen naturally. Remember to draw your tummy button in towards your spine. Let the breath in (your tummy should come out), then, when you're ready, start the next phrase. If there isn't much time to breathe, then shorten the first phrase to give yourself more time. Never snatch in the breath. Keep this cycle going through a whole song. Don't be tempted to top up the breath in between, or sneak in a little extra one.

Obviously, if there are significant spaces between phrases this will not apply. But remember always to breathe at least one whole beat before coming in when you start a song, new verse or wherever possible.

If you master this way of managing your breath, it will have a huge impact on your singing. You will be able to sing longer phrases, have much more control overall, and as a result your breathing, and therefore your body, will be relaxed.

If your breathing does become tight, breathe out hard a few times through your nose or mouth.

You will notice that as you gain more control over your breathing, you have to start to sing in a different way. If you are used to singing only short phrases and gasping in the air, it is hard to break this habit. You need consciously to make yourself sing longer phrases, otherwise, however good your general breath control has become, you will still continue to take in too much air through constant 'topping up'.

You will need to challenge yourself – bad singing habits can be very hard to overcome. This does not mean you have to alter your phrasing: just avoid breathing in all the gaps. Only take in air when you need to – use up your air first.

This can be a tricky thing to get your head around initially. It is difficult to believe that by breathing less frequently you will have more air, or breath, but it really is true. You will be amazed how much more control you will have.

Handy tip: If you are running out of breath at the end of a phrase that's not too high in your voice, place the sound forward in the front of your mouth in a small almost 'oo' shape. This helps to slow the flow of air and can often get you through the phrase.

A good way to practice singing long phrases is to rehearse singing them mentally (i.e. without any sound). Put your hands low on your tummy. Breathe in. Now imagine you are singing the phrase. Let the air out as if you were singing, but don't make any sound. If your breath can last for the whole phrase, you are ready to sing it properly. I find it helps to focus on the breath if I keep my eyes closed, as I internalise my thoughts more easily this way.

Another good exercise is to practice with a metronome. Set it to a fairly slow speed, about 1 beat at 60 bpm. Sing a single held note on 'ah' or 'ee' for a count of 6, breathe for a count of 1 and then repeat. When you feel comfortable with this gradually increase the speed. Take it as fast as you can manage. It's such a great way of focusing on the breath. Be careful not to breathe for 2 beats; you'll be surprised how tempting it is.

CHAPTER 12 SUMMARY

- Learning to sing 'on the vowel' is a pivotal moment in the lives of most singers.

- When you sing, you can only really hold notes on vowel sounds.

- The main vowel sounds used in singing are: **'ah'** as in heart, **'awe'** (yawn), **'oh'** (got), **'o'** (low), **'oo'** (moo), **'i'** (lid), **'ee'** (tree), **'uh'** (shut), and **'e'** (met).

- In order to sing in a *legato* (smooth or 'joined-up') way you need to be able to sing through every vowel.

- Consonants are important in their own right: for making the words clear, and for percussive effect.

- In order to achieve 'groove' and line in your singing you need to learn how to 'spring off' consonants onto vowels.

- You should focus on the out-breath when you sing a song.

- You should aim to breathe in as soon as you have used up the air – never 'snatch' in the air.

- If there isn't much time to breathe between phrases then shorten the first phrase to give yourself more time.

- Keep a natural cycle of breath going and don't be tempted to 'top up' the breath within phrases or steal extra ones.

Chapter 13
Style And Phrasing

I have covered how you make the sound and how to vary and enhance its quality. Now it's time to tackle singing actual songs. I want you to understand what makes certain singers special. Yes, it's partly down to the sound or quality of their voice and the material they sing, but the root of their success lies in what they do with the sound once they have made it. It is not only how they sing the words that is important, but where they 'put' them. Is the singer, for example, behind the beat, on it, or in front of it? Let me explain.

Feel

The songs that stay with us are those that move us in some way – they have energy, emotion or both. Delivering a song is not just about singing a correct melody and lyric in a technically perfect way. It is also about interpretation, style and what we call 'feel'. The singing has to be convincing: we need to feel the singer is emotionally involved or 'believes' in the sentiment of the song for us to get involved as a listener.

A singer's impact depends on their interpretation of a song. If the song were sung as it is written in a songbook, it would sound 'straight' and lifeless. There are many different elements involved in putting across a song well.

A singer, in order to add meaning or colour, may pick out certain words for emphasis by varying their rhythm, lengthening or shortening them, giving them more weight, embellishing them in various ways or, in contrast, almost 'speaking' them. But when we talk about interpretation we are not solely concerned with what we do with the words or with raw emotion.

When you listen to a good singer you are aware, both consciously and unconsciously, that everything sounds just right. The best singers appear to be able to put a song across with ease. This does not happen by accident. Like any instrumentalist, these singers will have listened to hundreds of other singers over the years. Many will have borrowed licks or phrasing from their own favourites, tried out lots of ideas and, gradually, have become confident enough to develop their own individual style or feel.

Singing On/Off The Beat

Singers, not being machines, never sing perfectly on the beat. These small imperfections of timing, whether ahead or behind the beat, lie at the root of what we call 'feel'. Singers can make a song more exciting and interesting by varying the rhythmical phrasing – by starting words or phrases earlier ('pushing') or later ('sitting behind the beat').

While vocal melodies are frequently sung 'across the beat', it can at times be very effective to sing some lines pointedly bang on the beat for percussive impact. An interesting exercise is to listen to a track with a metronome click. You will be able to hear exactly where the stresses are coming. It is the rhythm of the singing that gives it its groove.

Developing good feel relies on extending your musical vocabulary. Start by listening closely to your favourite singers. Notice where they vary a repeated melody – say in a second verse or a final chorus – maybe by simply taking it higher. If the line is repeated in an identical way, the impact isn't the same.

> **KEY POINT**
>
> *Good singers will vary the rhythmical phrasing of a song by singing before, behind or dead on the beat. This lies at the root of what we call 'feel'.*

Also listen for changes to the rhythm of a phrase: some words may be stretched or shortened. As we have seen, you need to be aware when a singer is singing across the beat or when they are right on it. The singer has to consider the rhythm not only of the music but also of the words. The best singers really listen and react to the accompanying instruments and are rhythmically locked into the track.

At this point it is worth mentioning the importance of timing your breath correctly. If the breath is late, then your entry will be late. You should aim to take a breath approximately one beat before entry (this will prevent you from 'snatching' in the breath). You need to make space to breathe. You have to breathe in the right place in order not to 'throw' a phrase. Come off a line or phrase early to give yourself time to breathe, in the faster sections of a song (see *Breathing For Singing*, page 20).

Incidentally, the ends of words and phrases should always be rhythmic and never sloppy. If you end phrases crisply, this maintains the energy of the song. Even in slow ballads, the placing of the consonants adds to the overall feel of the song.

I have had the great privilege of working with James Morrison. In terms of feel he is one of the best in the business. He spent years listening to Stevie Wonder amongst others and totally immersed himself in music. You can hear this in his wonderful, golden, soulful voice. His interpretation of a song is always captivating, and his energy and commitment is hugely impressive. Every time he sings he gives 100%, even in rehearsals. I have to say when he's playing guitar and singing in my music room it always reminds me I <u>do</u> have the best job in the world!

Dynamics

Dynamics are the variations in volume – the 'louds' and 'softs' – a singer chooses to use for effect. They are the key to the 'build' of a song – if you like, its emotional 'shape'. Good singers think about dynamics and use them effectively.

The simplest dynamic pattern for a song is one that starts off softly and then builds to a loud climax. A more subtle shape might take the form of a quiet start, followed by a dynamic build, followed by a small drop, and ending with a big 'up'. You don't, however, always have to sing a high note loudly or end a song full 'belt' – in fact, the opposite can be very effective. Consider Beyonce's *If I Were A Boy*. The song has a great build and big choruses, and there

KEY POINT

Singers use dynamics – 'louds' and 'softs' – to help create the emotional shape of a song.

is a lot of ad-libbing over the final chorus. However, Beyonce brings the singing right down to end the song sensitively and with real intensity.

Singers of classical music or other score-written music will, of course, be familiar with dynamic instructions such as *forte* (loud), *piano* (soft), *crescendo* (get louder), *diminuendo* (get softer) etc, but to what degree the individual singer responds to these suggestions is still to a certain extent up to interpretation. Some innately musical singers will interpret the same piece of music far more powerfully than others.

In popular music it is through improvising or ad-libbing that a singer makes a song his or her own. Improvisation can range from changing a word or a line, to changing whole phrases and introducing new ones. For your improvisation to sound convincing you have to be confident and bold (see *Improvisation*, page 100).

CHAPTER 13 SUMMARY

- In addition to singing a song well technically, delivering a song has a lot to do with interpretation, style and 'feel'.

- Small imperfections of timing, whether ahead or behind the beat, lie at the root of what we call 'feel'.

- Good singers vary the rhythmical phrasing of a song for emotional effect.

- The singer has to consider the rhythm not only of the music but also of the words.

- Dynamics are the 'louds' and 'softs' a singer chooses to use for effect. Their use helps to create the emotional shape of a song.

Chapter 14
Improvisation

The term *improvisation* as it is used here refers to the way an individual singer chooses to embellish or make excursions from the original melody of a song. It is the means by which the singer interprets a song in their own way.

Billie Holiday was arguably one of the most influential singers of the last century. It is said of her that she never sang any song the same way twice. Her interpretation was second to none. She had the ability to make a song her own by altering its melody and phrasing, and thereby its emotional complexity and impact.

Many of you reading this book may not have aspirations to be great jazz singers, but it is the development of jazz and blues singing that lies at the heart of improvisation in many forms of music. It is fair to say improvisation came naturally to the likes of Billie Holiday, and it is precisely this that worries certain people. Whilst some may view themselves as quite decent singers, they don't necessarily see themselves as natural improvisers.

Even Billie Holiday, however, listened to a great deal of music and learned about improvisation through experience and experimentation. In this section I am going to suggest some practical things you can try to get you started – there are indeed elements of interpretation you can learn and begin to build into your singing.

You sometimes hear songs sung – regardless of musical style – the same way throughout, without any variations of phrasing or melody. It can produce pretty dull results. It is invariably more interesting and exciting if the singer 'lets go' a little, and, say, takes the chorus higher or puts in some ad-libs.

The majority of rock and pop songs follow a similar format. Commonly, a first verse will be sung 'straight', the second with some small embellishment, and the final verse taken higher. Sometimes this final verse will be taken quite a long way from the original melody. The choruses gradually build in a similar way.

If the idea of improvising fills you with dread, don't worry too much. Improvisation doesn't have to mean amazing Kurt Elling-type scatting or Beyoncé-style licks. There are various different ways you can improvise. At the heart of improvisation is the ability to take a song and alter the phrasing and/ or melody to personalise it, or 'make it your own'. This applies to jazz as well as rock and pop music.

The first step towards improvising is to listen closely to a lot of good singers. Tap out the beat of a song. Work out whether the singer is singing behind the beat, on the beat, or ahead of it. It is surprising what you can hear when you really focus in.

Now listen to the melody. Does the singer vary it at all and, if so, in what way? Do they alter just the odd word or whole phrases? Do they take sections higher or lower?

Once you have begun to work out what other singers do, you can start to have a go yourself.

Sing the first line of a song. Experiment by changing the rhythm of the words slightly. Try delaying the word on the second beat, for example; then try it dead on the beat, and then slightly before the beat. Now have a go on other words. Keep the variations you like. It is important to be able to 'pull' the words around. You need to feel you have control of the song, and that you don't have to sing every phrase exactly 'as written'.

Now try a verse and a chorus using this same approach, sometimes laying back behind the beat, and sometimes 'pushing' the singing on. Mix it up: sing some lines slowly; speed through others a little more quickly; vary the pace. Sometimes the meaning of the words will suggest whether to sing them fast or slow.

Different styles of music are characterised by particular approaches. For example, the typically laid-back feel of a blues song is achieved by singing predominantly behind the beat. In faster rock music you might sing slightly ahead of the beat to drive the music forward and add to the excitement or vibe.

Many people focus only on the sound they are producing when they work on their singing. However, rhythm is a vital element too. A singer can sing the most beautiful melody, but if they have a poor sense of rhythm the song becomes lifeless and will not engage the listener.

This is just as important in classical singing. Indeed I heard Bryn Terfyl, the wonderful Welsh baritone, say that Sir George Solti once punched the rhythm of a piece out so hard on his arm that it left him with bruises. If nothing else, it goes to show that sometimes you have to suffer for your art!

Take things one step at a time. When you start to feel more comfortable with the rhythm and phrasing, you can experiment and try taking 'risks' with the melody.

Ideally, you should know the original tune inside out before you start to move away from it. Many people think they know a song well, but it is only when they come to sing it without any help from the original recording they discover they don't. They may only, in fact, have a 'sketchy' idea, perhaps only really knowing a couple of lines of the verse and most of the chorus.

> *Now sing a line. Hold the last note and move it up, then try again, moving it down. It's simple really. Just choose another note that fits with the chord. Altering the last note of a phrase is probably the most common form of improvisation.*

Even if you don't understand the harmonic structure of a song, by listening closely and singing along to it, you will be able to work out which notes fit with the chords and which don't. The more securely you have the chord structure and harmony in your head the better.

> *If you play piano or guitar, play the chords from a familiar song. Now start on a mid-range note. Sing all the words on this one note. When you change chord, if this note doesn't fit, try moving it up or down just one semitone or*

tone. Go through the song, keeping the movement this economical. In this way you get right 'inside' the harmony.

Now sing the verse and alter the end of each line, making up your own tune to fit with the chords. Extend this to the chorus and the other verses. You are now improvising.

Another great way to practice is to play a blues progression and sing over it. Start with short phrases, just a few notes, gradually extending the rhythmic patterns and melody. This type of improvisation should feel like a musical journey or story, with a beginning, a middle and an end.

Because blues songs are based around a simple harmonic pattern, they are very good vehicles for improvisation. Anybody who has improvised blues on the guitar or piano, for example, will identify with what I said earlier about the excitement created by 'sitting behind the beat' or 'pushing'. In fact, a singer's improvisations quite often imitate guitar lines – for example, when 'bending' notes.

Good improvisation relies on a solid technique. The more adventurous you become, the more flexible your voice will have to be. Changing between registers will have to be smooth, for example.

But improvisation is not a question of pure inspiration: largely the ideas upon which it is based can be found in the melody, lyrics and instrumentation of the song.

Often it is structured around instrumental ideas found in a song, such as guitar or piano riffs. Small, improvised ideas based on these would be used more as fillers or ad-libs in instrumental sections or at the end of a song. They are usually sung on sounds such as 'mm', 'ah' or 'whoah', with the singer using their voice like an instrument (for example, by bending or sliding).

There are endless other forms of improvisation. A singer may choose at times to drop the lead and improvise over the backing vocals. They might 'answer' a BV (backing vocal). At other times a singer might select only a few words from the chorus to work with and add their own variations.

In an outro (the end section of a song), an experienced singer will take short, musical excursions in which they will develop some of the original phrases and introduce new musical ideas – often with strong, repeated, rhythmic patterns. These might involve sounds rather than words. A clichéd, imported lyric such as 'baby… I say baby!' still works amazingly well, largely because it is there for rhythmic rather than lyrical effect.

For jazz improvisation you can start by trying many of the things above. This is how I learned. As you get more advanced you need to know about the different scales and modes, but this is something beyond the scope of this particular book.

Nobody really sings songs totally 'straight'. This is largely because everyone has been influenced by the singers they listen to and like. Often without realising, they have taken on board all sorts of stylistic embellishments. In fact, listening to the phrasing and stylistic effects of the singers you like is the best thing you can do. If you don't feel confident about improvising, it is a great idea to start by copying the improvisations of those who are good at it. As your own musical vocabulary and confidence grow, the more you will feel the urge to step out on your own. It can be great fun, so get started – you may surprise yourself!

Shredders

This is a term used by guitar players for really flashy, speedy playing. Guitarists capable of great 'shredding' include the brilliant Eddie Van Halen and Steve Vai. These guys have practiced technique for hours and hours to get themselves up to virtuoso standard – their agility and dexterity are awesome. There are also singers for whom this is the case.

Many R&B singers are particularly known for their vocal agility and the effect can be very exciting (if it isn't overdone). Beyoncé is a great example, flashing up and down with her sparkling R&B licks.

One of the most agile (and golden) voices I have come across is Craig David's. I was lucky enough to work with Craig when he did his first two tours.

As part of a warm-up and as a means of strengthening his voice I used fast-moving articulation exercises. I have never known a voice to move as quickly as Craig's. I could not possibly keep up with him on the piano. Not only does his voice move ridiculously quickly, but every single note is absolutely spot on in pitch and very even in tone. His flexibility and accuracy are quite extraordinary. He is truly, in the best sense, a 'shredder' of the vocal world.

Few voices are capable of moving as quickly as Craig David's. His voice is extremely light and agile; other singers have weightier voices. Take Steven Tyler or Bruce Springsteen, for example. Their voices are heavier and they just wouldn't sound right doing fast riffs. It is no coincidence, of course, that their voices suit their material.

However, if you work at it you can improve agility, and I shall be giving you some exercises to help later in the book.

R&B Licks

R&B music is an extremely popular form. Many singers who come to me want, in particular, to improve their agility and their 'riffing' and 'licks'.

The best way to work on this is to listen closely to an artist you admire and try to copy their licks. Don't be over-ambitious. Choose one lick at a time. Listen to it several times, then try repeating it. Slow it down. If that is not working, sketch it out. You can do this by drawing a line with a pencil on a piece of paper that follows the shape of the lick. Does it go up or down, start high then go low etc?

To achieve the flexibility you need to for the riffs, it can help to place the sound forward. Remember, this means thinking of the sound ringing around the front of your face and head. If your voice is too open at the back, there will probably be too much weight in it and you won't be able to get it moving quickly enough.

Getting to be good at riffing is really down to practice. Many singers appear to be naturally good at it. This is because they have listened to a lot of R&B

music and have learned the 'language'. There is no doubt you can improve your riffing if you work at it, although some singers will find it more difficult than others because of the type of voice they possess.

R&B And The Gospel Tradition

Many R&B singers borrow from the great Gospel-singing tradition whose own roots lie in traditional African music and the spirituals and Black church music arising from the slavery era in the United States. The origins and significance of Gospel music are complex but many take the work of Mahalia Jackson and her contemporaries in the 1940s and 50s as the starting point of modern Black Gospel singing.

While they may be difficult to define in simple terms, the Black Gospel sound and style are instantly recognisable. The singing features great emotional intensity, as one would expect from a form of music inextricably linked to a declaration of Black selfhood and passionate Christian spirituality and faith.

It also features extravagant improvisation and ornamentation. There is often a 'call and answer' between the soloist and the choir (or the preacher and his congregation), echoing traditional Black 'field hollers' and other working songs. As a matter of fact, you often hear this 'call and answer' in popular singing, especially the Blues, and particularly within improvised BVs.

Although religious in origin, Gospel music has, undoubtedly, greatly influenced today's popular music forms and styles. Indeed, Soul music was one of the earliest popular forms that evolved largely from the Gospel tradition. Many leading soul artists began their musical careers as Gospel singers or accompanists in Baptist, Methodist or Pentecostal churches. The list includes, amongst others, James Brown, Aretha Franklin, Ray Charles, Lou Rawls, Sam Cooke and Otis Reading.

The Gospel singing style is a real performer's art. It is a method of delivering lyrics so demanding in terms of vocal skill and technique that performing it, like jazz, is highly spontaneous and intuitive in approach. In other words, not just anyone can do it!

The ornamentation used by Gospel singers seems to me totally appropriate to the form and spiritual sentiment of the music being expressed. What matters is a down-to-earth sincerity and heart-felt identification with the message of the song or hymn. My own view, however, is that whilst its influence on popular R&B singing is beyond question, adopting the ornamentation, style and phrasing of spiritual and Gospel singing without its technical expertise and sensitivity, can result in a kind of 'phoney' or shallow style of singing – what I call 'style over substance'.

Style-Over-Substance Singing

This approach to singing has unfortunately become very popular, especially among young singers. You only have to listen to the auditionees on shows like *American Idol*, *The Voice* or *The X Factor*. In an attempt to impress the judges, many of them try to add as many licks as possible within any given song. To be fair, they normally only have a very short time in which to catch the eyes and ears of the judges and so the temptation is understandable.

It is true that many R&B artists riff a lot but I'm not a fan of overdoing it to the point where the original melody of the song is rarely referred to. I like to hear the original melodic and emotional heart of a song coming through.

Unfortunately, many singers determined to sing in this way also happen to sing completely out of tune and/or have no idea about improvising around the chords of the song. This style of singing can also disguise poor technique and lack of breath control. Phrases can be very clipped, the singing too 'breathy', and all too often the singers are incapable of sustaining notes of any length.

Style-over-substance singers appeal to those who are fooled into thinking or, should we say, are prepared to believe that fancy licks and agility = great singing. These singers have all the 'style' or what you might call the 'surface features' of a particular genre – the phrasing and the licks, for example. But, sadly, many have no real technique, musical line, emotional quality, or genuine musicality – all the things that are ultimately rewarding to the listener. When I hear their vocal pyrotechnics I am always reminded of the old phrase, *never mind the quality, feel the width*.

I believe in getting 'inside' and finding a person's individual or 'real' voice, discovering what makes them tick, and bringing out their uniquely individual qualities when they sing. All successful artists with any longevity have a real identity which 'speaks' to you. It comes from within; it is not something 'painted on'.

It is important, of course, to have freedom in your singing and to have your own style. Bringing your own inflections to a melody will bring it to life. Indeed, as I have said before, it would be boring if singers stuck rigidly to the melody all the way through a song. However, improvising should be an organic process, and the results should be 'meaningful' and musical – not just a matter of fitting in as many notes as possible in order to impress.

---

*Ornamentation has long been used to decorate and embellish music. The **cadenza** is the name given to a brilliant solo passage performed by a solo voice or instrumentalist. It appears near the end of an aria or movement of a concerto. It is a great showpiece for singers. It was introduced by Italian opera singers in the late 17th century and soon after that in Germany. The original idea was that it should last no longer than a single breath and should end with a trill.*

CHAPTER 14 SUMMARY

- Some singers are natural improvisers, but there are many aspects of improvisation you can learn.

- You can start by experimenting with changes in the rhythm and phrasing of a song, and then go on to varying the melody.

- Many of the ideas upon which improvisation is based can be found in the melody, lyrics and instrumentation of the song.

- To achieve the flexibility you need for agile R&B riffs, it can help to place the sound forward.

- Guard against adopting the ornamentation, style and phrasing of Gospel singing unless you have the technique to do it justice.

- Your own improvisation should be meaningful and musical – not just a matter of fitting in as many notes as possible in order to impress.

Chapter 15
Tuning

How important is it to sing in tune? What do we mean by perfect pitch or relative pitch? What is meant by the term 'tone deaf', and if you struggle with tuning, how can you improve it? In this section we will examine the often-neglected yet vital issues around singing in tune.

Am I Tone Deaf?

I constantly hear people being written off as singers by others – and equally often by themselves – on the grounds that they are irredeemably 'tone deaf'. But what is really meant by the expression and is it so cut and dried?

Many people are so resigned to the idea of being 'tone deaf' that they rarely sing in case someone laughs at them. The sad fact is many people with real hang-ups about tone-deafness have a secret and passionate desire to sing. I believe it is really unfair and damaging to make fun of someone's singing. Apart from anything else, self-confidence is a huge factor in being able to sing to the best of one's ability. In addition, I would like to say a few things about out-of-tune singing and explain why there may yet be hope for even the most extreme cases.

There are a number of reasons why people have tuning problems, but these often derive from negative childhood or teenage experiences. Many adults I know don't sing because at the age of seven or eight they were not chosen for the school choir or were teased and made to believe they had hopeless voices. This has been enough to put them off for life.

It is true, unfortunately, that some people do have a problem singing in tune – and some more than others. As I said, there are many reasons for this and they may not be quite what you would expect.

I always feel the expression 'tone deaf' is a little harsh. It is used to describe a singer who sings totally and consistently out of tune – something which in actual fact is quite a difficult thing to achieve: invariably, even the worst cases seem to hit some of the correct notes some of the time.

The term 'tone deaf' seems to suggest something fixed and unalterable, since surely if you are 'deaf' there is nothing you can do about it. However, in my experience, even the most hopeless-sounding cases can to a certain extent be rescued. It may take some time, but it is achievable!

Most people have a reasonable sense of pitch. Commonly, however, many people experience pitching problems when trying to sing either too high or too low. They can be bang in tune in the middle of their voice, but as they move up or down their voices begin to tense up. The muscles around the larynx clamp down and prevent the vocal cords from vibrating freely to produce the correct pitch. With the right technique these singers can learn to remove this tension. As a result they can begin to sing more reliably in tune whatever the pitch.

Some people start off a song on the right note but their tuning wanders as it progresses. This is usually due to their lack of musical experience. For singers like this I recommend they take up an instrument as this will help to train their ears to listen or 'hear' properly.

Strangely enough if you give people the instruction to 'listen', suddenly they can become more accurate. It's almost as if they have forgotten or never learned how to listen closely to their own voices or the musical accompaniment.

If you can pick out a simple melody on a keyboard, singing along will reinforce your sense of pitch. If you can play the chords to a song whilst picking out the melody, this will help train your ear even more effectively.

Make sure you are singing notes that fit with the chord you are playing and don't clash. This may sound obvious, but believe me many people don't do it.

There are physical reasons why some people sing out of tune. Adults who have never really sung before will have singing muscles which are 'flabby' and in need of toning up. Other causes include unwanted tension in the jaw area, or 'collapsing' of the body (see pages 41). As we have seen before, how you use your body affects your voice, and with some people the effect on tuning can be extreme.

For some reason, people who have difficulty singing in tune often have a poor sense of rhythm too. An old friend of mine was one such person. Giving up all hope of a singing career, he joined the army and found he couldn't even march in time!

The most challenging case I have ever encountered was that of a woman in her early thirties. She had an exceptionally deep voice and had experienced many vocal problems. She had a range of only a 3rd (three notes) and produced a sort of 'droning' sound as she attempted to move up and down the scale. There was a huge amount of tension surrounding her jaw, throat, chest and shoulders. We began with songs that had a small range and with very careful and gradual work she increased her range to an octave and a half, and her tuning became very good. She also learnt an instrument at the same time and this really helped her. She may never be an amazing singer but she can now hold a tune and make a perfectly acceptable sound – and she loves it!

Due to vocal misuse some very good singers can find themselves developing tuning problems. The upsetting thing is they can hear they are singing out of tune but find they can do little to change it. They have to either push their voices, particularly in the upper middle part, or sing very quietly to get the pitch anywhere near accurate. This kind of problem is often a warning sign for the development of nodules (see page 181). If this is happening, I would seriously recommend having a check-up and singing lessons from a good teacher.

If you are having pitching problems, particularly as you go higher, it is worth thinking about the notes being three-dimensional. Imagine a note having a bottom, a middle and a top. If you're singing flat, for example, it's almost as if you're only singing with the bottom and the middle of the note and not enough top, or upper resonance. If you imagine adding the upper resonance, or top third dimension on to the note it can have an amazing effect.

Perfect Pitch

This is the term used for the ability certain people have to recognise and name a note on first hearing. People with perfect pitch can also sing any note within their range unaccompanied.

I have perfect pitch and it's something I think I was born with. You are unlikely to know you have perfect pitch unless you have learned an instrument. Having it can be useful but, as I will explain, not always. It is certainly no indication of 'musicality', or whether you are a good singer or not.

Having said this, it does seem to develop in relation to the instrument you play. I play the piano and could tell you any note played on the piano with 100% success. However, my pitch is not quite as reliable with stringed instruments, which suggests there is certainly also a learned element.

The disadvantage comes when you are sight-reading music. Generally speaking, having perfect pitch helps you, but if the key changes you have to start transposing (put the music into a different key) on the spot. This has happened to me in the past when I have been singing something quite complex with a group, unaccompanied. As a piece progresses, the pitch might drop a tone or so; I then end up having to transpose as I am reading. It can be scary!

Don't worry if you don't have perfect pitch, neither do most professional singers.

Relative Pitch

On the other hand, most musicians have this. Relative pitch is the ability to pitch notes from a given starting note. In other words, you can hear the relationship between the notes of a melody (the intervals) and be able to sing 'in tune with yourself' from any given starting point. Relative pitch is learned through practice. People who sing regularly, even though they may not have perfect pitch, will eventually develop a feel for whether they are more or less in the right key or on the right note.

Singing In Tune

So how important is it to be able to sing in tune consistently? I imagine most of you would agree with me and reply 'very', but you may be surprised how often I have had arguments with people in the music industry about this.

Because of the development of digital tuning programmes such as *Autotune* and *Melodyne* we are used to hearing most recorded vocals sounding well in tune. This is obviously good news for us as listeners, but singers sometimes struggle to maintain good tuning when singing live. Clearly there are many absolutely superb singers out there, but for a substantial number of artists tuning doesn't appear to be a priority.

Poor tuning is definitely more accepted in rock and pop than it is, say, in jazz, show or classical singing. Yet it is interesting to note that in no other area of rock and pop musicianship would these lax standards be tolerated.

Having said that, I appreciate when singing live there are often genuine reasons for bad tuning beyond a singer's control. For example, singers often have difficulty hearing themselves on stage due to issues relating to the PA and how well the music is mixed and monitored for them. I also concede a certain amount of out-of-tune singing is acceptable within the context of live rock and pop performance, where 'feel', stage presence and excitement can take priority.

Most artists of a certain level performing on TV or live use in-ear monitors so they can hear themselves clearly. They will get an individual mix of their own voice plus either a backing track or, if singing with a band, a mix of instruments. They can choose the level of each instrument or track and which instruments they want to hear. Some singers only like a little bit of keyboards or guitar or bass, some like to have a mix of everything. The monitors are so sophisticated now that they can even have a mix of the audience allowing the singer to get more of a live 'vibe'. Also, as they can hear themselves, it really helps with tuning.

Overall, though, I believe the ability to sing in tune is a basic requirement of any singer. Nobody should expect perfect tuning all the time – the vast majority of singers will not hit every note of a song bang on (although the best ones can hear when they are slightly out and make quick adjustments), but consistently out-of-tune singing is clearly unacceptable.

The reasons behind the continued acceptance of poor vocal standards (including poor tuning) and a related resistance to vocal coaching are complex and varied. Things have improved in recent years: more singers are taking their singing seriously and really working at it.

The importance of image and looks in contemporary pop music, boosted by the popularity of 'fame wannabe' shows, has led to a crop of singers who, not to put too fine a point on it, have little in the way of technique and often an inability to sing in tune consistently.

Many of the 'created' artists rely too heavily on studio production and techniques to hide their technical inadequacies. What sets the 'genuine' artists apart from the others is their ability to sing and perform well *live* and that includes singing in tune.

What Key Do I Sing In?

This is something people ask me all the time. It may sound a perfectly reasonable question, but in fact it doesn't make any sense. Let me explain.

You can sing in *any* key – it just depends where the melody you want to sing lies within that key. In other words, the highest or lowest notes of the song must be within your range.

Take, for example, the key of C Major. The notes in the scale are C, D, E, F, G, A, B and C. In G Major the notes of the scale are G, A, B, C, D, E, F sharp and G. You can see from this that both scales share the same notes except that G has an F sharp where C has an F.

All the major and minor scales share the same notes, except the sharps and flats vary depending on the key you are in.

Whether you can sing a song in any one key depends on which notes are in the tune and how high (or low) they go. A high C or G may make the song too high for you. A tune that only uses mid-range Cs and Gs would be easier to sing. As you can see from the examples, these notes appear in both the G and C scales. Therefore, it doesn't make any sense to say, 'I can only sing in G, not C.'

If a song has a high B or G, and you can only manage a high E or C, you will need to transpose or lower the key of the song by a 5th. This would take the B down to E and the G down to C.

Alternatively, if the low notes of a song are too low, you will need to transpose up. If the lowest note you feel comfortable singing is a D and the lowest note of the song is a low A, you will need to raise the key by a 4th.

Keys are funny things, though. Some songs just don't sound right sung in certain keys – we know from experience, for example, that some keys sound naturally 'brighter' than others.

In addition, many musicians write songs in G and C, since the common (open) chords in these keys are familiar. G is a common and important note in both these keys. The problem many singers have is that a high G is just about at the top of their range. Choruses in these two keys, in particular, are often written around high Gs and can become very tiring for your voice. I have some suggestions to help you with this.

Obviously, the easiest option for the singer is to lower the key, but it may well just not be practical for you or the band. If your band is covering or has written and rehearsed a song, and has spent ages working out riffs or guitar solos, the last thing you want to have to do is change the key. Some singers opt for tuning the guitars down a semi tone.

The next option is to use alternative melody notes, taking a lower harmony, for example. If you were singing a G over a G chord, you could replace it with a D (the 5th of the chord). Alternatively, if you were singing a G over a C chord, you could replace it with an E (the 3rd of the chord).

I hope this doesn't sound too mind-boggling – it's really simpler than it seems initially. If you play around with these ideas on a keyboard or guitar I think you will soon get the idea.

Another way around the problem for men (at the top) is to sing in falsetto. Now I know, as previously stated, many people think falsetto singing is a weaker-sounding option, but if you have a nice bunch of harmonies going on as well, it can sound really good. An additional advantage of using falsetto is that it will help prevent you from wrecking your voice!

Singing High

Correct use of head voice is the real answer to sustaining a high melody. As we have seen, the problem many of you will have is taking your chest voice too high. Remember *chest voice* is the term used to describe the place you resonate the sound when you sing lower notes. As you sing up the scale, the feeling of the resonance should move gradually into your head (*head voice*). If you don't allow this to happen, you will 'push' the top of your voice too much, eventually leading to strain (see *Registers*, page 69).

Don't forget, if you do transpose a song down and sing it in a lower key than the original, it doesn't mean you are a poorer singer. Some people naturally have higher or lower voices than others.

CHAPTER 15 SUMMARY

- A certain amount of out-of-tune singing is acceptable, especially when singing live, but consistently singing out of tune needs addressing.

- Few people are genuinely 'tone deaf' – with practice most people can learn to sing in tune.

- There are a number of reasons why people have tuning problems, but something can be done about most of them.

- Perfect Pitch is the ability to instantly recognise and name a played note, or the ability to sing any named note accurately.

- Relative Pitch is the ability to pitch notes from a given starting note.

- Theoretically, you can sing in *any* key, as long as the highest or lowest notes of the particular song are within your range.

- Correct use of head voice is the real answer to sustaining a high melody.

Chapter 16
Singing Exercises

Why Do Singing Exercises?

Working with singing exercises is an integral part of any program designed to develop a good singing technique. Whatever style of music you sing, they are hugely important.

Having said that, I am afraid many so-called singing coaches use singing exercises in an entirely arbitrary way, often without understanding how a particular exercise might help the singer.

For this reason I have added notes to the recommended exercises below that aim to explain their usefulness.

If you apply all the main principles outlined in this book your singing should really improve. However, working with singing exercises will not only help you develop your voice, it will also help you gain a real awareness of how you should be using it.

There are many benefits to be gained from working with singing exercises regularly. These include: improving breath control; strengthening your voice; increasing your range; developing your tone and resonance; gaining understanding and control of your registers; and increasing vocal agility.

Practicing singing exercises regularly helps to develop appropriate *muscle memory*. The muscles involved in singing are used to responding, or are in the habit of responding, in certain ways when we sing. We can develop bad habits, for example, tensing our jaws and tongues, and tightening the muscles of our larynx. The idea of singing exercises is to stimulate your 'good' muscles to work so that you can let go of these tensions.

Different exercises work to develop different aspects of technique. As you practice, you are training your muscles to respond in a technically healthy way, and given time the old muscles will 'let go'.

Many singers worry if they do singing exercises they will start to sound like opera singers. Obviously, some of you will *want* to sound like opera singers. But if you don't want to sound like an opera singer, there is nothing to fear: *you* are the one in control of the sound you make when singing – through the choices you make around resonance, phrasing etc. In fact, it is more accurate to regard the benefits of singing exercises as giving you *more* choices in terms of the sound you produce.

The aim is to develop your voice into a strong, stable instrument with which you can 'play' any kind of music. Remember, virtually all kinds of singing rely on the same basic principles of technique. As you develop your voice, you will find you are able to do more things with it – it's an exciting idea.

Some singers initially find the thought of practicing with singing exercises quite daunting. It can feel totally alien to use one's voice in such an ordered way, having always sung 'instinctively' before. If this applies to you, don't be put off. Persevere with the exercises (especially when no one is listening!) and you will soon feel the benefits. Don't expect to do the exercises perfectly at first. In fact, it doesn't matter how long you have been singing, you can always get a bit more out of an exercise. As is the case in other areas of your life, you can never stop learning and developing.

It is better to go through exercises with an experienced teacher if possible, as she or he will help ensure you are not doing anything wrong. This being a self-help book, however, I am going to give you detailed notes on how to approach the exercises on your own. This will help you get the best out of them, ensure you only improve, and not run the risk of damaging your voice.

Exercises can also be used as a warm-up. If you are using them for this purpose, don't do too many and make sure you pace yourself – 10/15 minutes at a time may be enough for you initially (see *Warm Up*, page 186). You can do them in any order. Different things suit different people.

The exercises I am giving you are very much an individual selection. There are many more, but these represent a good start. In the general warm-up section I have set out some exercises you can do without the help of an instrument. All these warm-ups such as sirening are great for getting your voice going and can be used before you start the notated exercises.

The exercises I give you in this section are based around musical notation. If you don't read music, get a friend who plays keyboard or guitar (or any other suitable instrument) to record the basic shapes so you can practice them as much as you like. Alternatively, download my versions of the exercises to practice with.

All the suggestions for starting notes are very general. Start where you feel comfortable – it will depend on your voice type. Remember, never try to go too high or low. You shouldn't strain your voice doing exercises. Some singers like to start their exercises high and descend; others prefer it the other way round. Choose which feels best for you. It is suggested in each exercise that you move in semi-tones (half steps) up or down.

All the exercises (except for the 'vv') are sung on vowel sounds. The reason for this is, as I have said before, the singing sound only happens on the vowels and not the consonants (see *Singing On The Vowel*, page 90).

Sing the exercises at medium volume unless otherwise instructed. Don't sing them at the top of your voice – it will become too tiring. Sometimes you will want to let rip, and indeed it can be difficult to get the support going at first if the singing is too quiet.

The order of the given exercises is unimportant. Some will suit you more than others. Don't try all of them at once. Start with a few and gradually introduce some more. Some singers prefer to begin with the articulation exercises as they get your voice moving, but it's really up to you.

My Top Twenty Singing Exercises

An example of each of the following twenty exercises is given in the key of C. Suggestions for starting notes are given under each exercise. Simply repeat the exercise, moving up a semitone each time, but don't go too high that it gets uncomfortable. These exercises are available to download from my website.

Before you start it is a good idea to do some 'sirening' – sliding up and down the scale on a 'vv' or 'ng' sound. Always do it gently without too much breath pressure. Start low, sirening up and then down, or start high and finish low, whatever feels good.

1. 'Vee'

This is a great warm-up to get the support going. Put your hands below your tummy button and feel it springing in and engaging as you sing 'vee'. Sing 'vee' on each note up and down a five-note scale passage. Don't take it too high. It is good to practice this ascending and then descending.

Men: Start around G (an octave and a bit below Middle C). Only go as high as E or F below Middle C.

Women: Start on G below Middle C and only go as high D above Middle C.

2. Five-Note Scale passage

You can take this exercise a bit higher. It uses the same pattern as above, but start with a 'vee' and continue on the 'ee sound.

This is excellent for getting the forward resonance going. If you prefer, put a 'm' sound in front of the vowel – this also helps to 'trigger' the muscles you use to support your voice.

3. Triads

This exercise introduces you to thinking about your larynx moving down as you sing higher. For women it particularly helps with bringing the head voice lower and integrating it with the chest voice to sing with mixed register.

I sometimes prefer to start this higher and descend.

Sing this exercise in the same register as in exercises 1 and 2.

As you sing, imagine a see-saw moving down as the singing goes up. It feels a bit like you're stretching a piece of elastic; it's a two-way stretch, up and down. Allow the sound to drop into the front of your face and behind your eyes. Keep an open, lifted, 'smiley' space in the back of your mouth. The space gets more open as you sing the higher notes. Sing it on 'mee' and then 'ah'.

It may help when singing 'ah' to think of the sound starting slightly forward, to stop the sound getting too dark or stuck around your jaw.

4. Repeated Notes

This exercise has a number of benefits: it helps to tone up your vocal cords by getting them to come together properly, enabling you to start a note cleanly; it also helps to eliminate unwanted breathiness; and it is great for putting you in touch with your support muscles and getting the sound flowing through your body.

Do this exercise in the lower to middle part of your range.

Men: Start on D or D flat below Middle C, up in semitones to F, and then back down.

Women: Start the same as the men but an octave higher.

Sing the repeated notes first on 'ah'. This is a tricky exercise to get to grips with. Don't be tempted to sneak extra breath in; it should be sung in one breath. The exercise should flow from beginning to end, even though you keep stopping the sound. The key is to make sure the onset of each note is not 'glottal' – that means it shouldn't feel like it is starting from your throat. It's a bit like the feeling of stroking a cat. It should feel like you are 'leaning' down into the note. You lean down on the column of air. There is almost a feeling of resistance, but the sound moves further down the singing tube with each note.

Have your hands low down on your tummy. Remember to think about drawing your tummy button in towards your spine. Feel the tummy coming in with each note. Keep the muscle tension going in between each note; don't let your support go 'sloppy'. Also, be careful not to let any air out before the start of each note.

I use this exercise a lot, particularly if I've had a lay off due to a cold or cough. It is great for everyone, but especially those with any voice problems.

5.   Staccato Arpeggio

This exercise follows the same principles as the last. It works on support and the prevention of 'glottal attack'. Again, you shouldn't feel the onset of each note in your throat. As you go up, think down. Think of a lift moving down or a cafetière plunging down as you sing up. Make sure you draw in your tummy and support the upper note.

Men: Begin on G an octave and a bit below Middle C. Stop around E.

Women: The same range as men but an octave higher.

Make sure the singing feels 'connected' all the time. If it feels strained or pushed, stop. Staccato exercises can be very beneficial, but they are hard work and require lots of support.

Try it on 'mee' and 'ah'.

6.   Legato Arpeggio

This arpeggio exercise will help in smoothing out the transition from one register to another and give you a greater awareness of your registers – where they change and the difference between them. It also helps with both support and keeping a low larynx.

Think down and open as you sing up the scale. Remember your 'Cinderella dress'. Sing it on an 'ee' and 'ah'. You may want to put a 'm' before each vowel to help you anchor your support (making 'mee' and 'mah').

Keep the support going. Think of a combination of a downward movement and engaging your tummy a split second before you sing the high note. This gives you more chance to get the support working in addition to preventing your larynx from rising.

As you go higher, allow the sound to drop gradually into your head. It may help you to think of it being forward, dropping in behind your eyes or getting lighter. You should encourage the introduction of head voice into the sound. Think of the sound going up from behind your head and over the front of your face. This helps to allow your larynx to move forward and down when singing in head voice.

Start this in the same place as the previous exercise. Take it as high as feels comfortable. As you go higher open your mouth more, particularly inside. If it helps, put your fingers in 'the groove' (see page 36), and make sure your soft palate is lifting with a little, inner 'smile'.

As you take the sound higher, allow the resonance to come into the front of your head, but always keep the space open in the back of your throat (or mouth). It seems a bit confusing at first as you have to think in two directions simultaneously. It might help if you change the 'ee' to more of an 'i' (as in 'lid'). This will help to keep your larynx relaxed and give more depth to the sound.

7.   Arpeggio Plus Dominant 7th

This exercise is another good one for linking up the registers. It is also a useful 'ear trainer' as the descending pattern is slightly unpredictable.

Focus on the same elements of technique as you did in the previous exercise. Some people find this easier than the arpeggio as it is a bit freer-flowing.

Use the same range as above.

8.   Arpeggio Plus 10th

This is a slightly extended version of the arpeggio exercises. Sing it fairly quickly. I recommend the fingers in the 'groove' for this one.

Use the same range and vowels as before.

9.   Extended Arpeggio Plus Dominant 7th

This exercise is similar to the other arpeggio-based ones. It stretches you a bit further and it requires good control to be accurate on the way down. Thinking forward on the way down can help.

Make sure you open up at the top and allow the sound to drop in from above. Think down and open as you go higher.

Sing on the same vowels as in the previous exercise and start in the same place. Take it as high as is comfortable.

10. Five-note Scales And Triad Combined

This is a particularly good exercise for breath control, as it should last for about eight seconds in total. It also helps with the transition from one register to another and with the development, in particular, of your middle register. You can sing it on 'ee', 'ah' and 'oo'.

Start off singing in the middle of your voice. In time you can take it throughout your whole voice and it is a great strengthener. Don't open your mouth too wide at the bottom. Keep the sound 'focused', but still keep the space in the back of your throat.

Men: Start around C below Middle C. Take it up to about a G, so your highest note would be D. If it feels comfortable you can take it higher. You will need to introduce more head voice into the sound. When you get to E flat you should be singing with some head voice, and by the time you've reached F sharp it should be right in your head.

Women: Start in the same place as men but an octave higher. Allow the sound to begin moving into your head around E flat. This is where you can start thinking of singing with a mix of chest and head registers, which is known as your middle register. As you go higher, let the sound go more into your head. In the middle you want a real mix of chest and head registers.

Some singers find this exercise easier if they start higher and descend.

11. Held Single Notes

This exercise works on forward resonance and tone production. It also encourages you to be relaxed as you sing – both with your breath and in your body. This is such a useful place to explore as often, if you are short of breath, particularly when the singing isn't too high, by placing the sound here it will give you much more control and often gets you through to the end of a phrase.

Put your lips forward in an 'oo' shape with your top lip slightly more forward than the bottom. Sing a single mid to low-range note and hold it for the length of your breath. As you hold it, feel the resonance (buzz) ringing around the front of your face and top lip. Make sure your tongue is flat in your mouth and relaxed. Sing on 'oo'. Then sing 'ee' through your 'oo' shaped mouth. This is a very exaggerated position but is excellent for getting the forward resonance going.

Men: Start on F below Middle C and descend in semitones.

Women: Start an octave higher.

12. Five-note Run And Hold

This is an extension of the previous exercise and works on both resonance and forward placing.

You can start by trying the first example and work up to the second one. Sing it on 'oo' and 'ee'. The range is the same as in the previous exercise.

13. Five-note Run And Hold With Vowel Bend

This exercise works on resonance, placing and vowel unification (moving from one vowel to another smoothly).

The exercise is the same as the previous exercise, although as you hold the note you move from 'ee' to 'ai' (as in 'sail') to 'ah'. It is quite hard to do this smoothly. Don't move from one sound to the other by changing your mouth shape; alter them inside. You do it by lifting the stretchy soft palate. Each vowel should grow out of the previous one; there should be no sudden gear changes. Use the same range as above.

14. Rotating The Registers

This is an exercise for women. It is designed to help develop an awareness of the difference between chest voice and middle register, and to smooth out the changes. Sing the first three notes in chest voice and then the fourth note in middle register, ending the exercise in chest voice. The change to middle register is difficult, as you will already have sung the upper note in chest the first time. As you move into mixed register, think down. This will help you to keep your larynx low and relaxed. Also think of making the sound a bit lighter.

Start on A flat below Middle C and ascend in semitones (half steps) to the C above. Then come back down. As you practice this exercise you can gradually reduce the size of the interval you are singing from a major third to a second. For example, you start off rotating from C to E, then sing C to E flat, then C to D. This will help you develop control.

15. Octave Jumps – Rotating The Registers

This is another good exercise for women, but it also has its uses for men*. It is quite an advanced exercise; be careful not to overdo things. You sing the lower notes in chest voice or mixed register, and the upper notes in head voice.

Always remember to 'think down' and support as you sing up. Start on Middle C, ascending in semitones (half steps). Stop on the F or F sharp above. Each time you sing the upper note you will have to allow for an increasing amount of head resonance in the sound.

Depending on voice type, the sound will be in your head at C or C sharp above Middle C. As you go up it changes again around F or F sharp as it moves to a higher place in your head.

*Men can use this exercise to practice going from full voice into falsetto. Start on F below Middle C.

Sing it on 'ee' and 'ah'.

16. Articulation – Scale With Turnaround

This exercise will help you improve your vocal agility. The trick with articulation is not to try and sing every note. *Think* the notes as you sing and try not to have too much weight in your voice.

Some people's voices are naturally more agile than others, but you can improve your agility with practice.

Start with your mouth quite focused. It can help a lot if you sing with your fingers in the 'groove'. As you go higher, open your mouth more; keep the space in the back of your mouth and allow the sound to drop into the front of your head.

Keep the breath low and remember to support the sound, particularly at the top. It helps if you think of a slight emphasis on the first of every four notes. As you go higher always think down and open.

Men: Start on B below Middle C (if you have a low voice start on the G below). Go as high as feels comfortable.

Women: the same range but an octave higher.

Sing on 'ee' and 'ah'. You may find it easier to put a 'm' before each vowel. This helps to stop you attacking the starting note from your glottis. It softens the onset of the vowel, takes pressure off your vocal cords, and helps to get you connected to the support.

17. Articulation

This is a similar exercise to the previous one but the patterns are different. You will probably find the singing feels easier on the way down. The reason for this is that once you have reached the top you will have established your head voice; then as you descend you will automatically sing with more head voice. On the way up you may drag the chest voice too high if you are not careful. Breathe before descending.

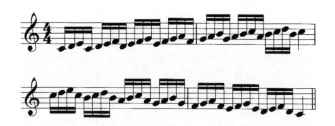

You can think of this exercise as a '1231' pattern (in piano fingering) because you sing the 1st note of the scale, then the 2nd, then the 3rd, before returning to the 1st. To take this exercise further you can vary the pattern. Try: a) 1321 b) 3213 c) 1243.

Sing on the same vowels as above, in the same register.

18. Octave Plus Descending Scale

This is a lovely one to sing and again is generally easier for women.

Follow all the previous instructions for articulation exercises. As you sing the octave leap, think down and support. As you sing the upper notes, swing your arms out to the sides of the room. It gives you a great feeling of freedom as well as making it easier to sing.

Start on Middle C and take it as high as is comfortable. Sing on a 'mee' and a 'mah'.

19. Combination Exercise

This is a very advanced exercise that combines some of the previous articulation exercises. It is technically very challenging. Use the same principles, the same vowels, and start on the notes as in the other articulation exercises. Only do this one if you're feeling on top of your game!

20. Falsetto Exercises

This is an exercise for men. It will strengthen your falsetto and help to get rid of any unwanted breathiness.

Sing the five-note pattern (from Exercises 1/2) in falsetto. Keep the breath relaxed. You want a feeling of stillness in your body as you sing this. Don't try to force the sound out. Stay calm.

Sing first on 'moo', then 'mee' and 'mah'. Keep the space in the back of your mouth, but place the notes very forward in your head and the front of your face around your nose (but don't make the sound nasal). Keep your mouth focused.

You may find the 'mah' more difficult and breathy. Keep it focused and try to slot it into the same place as the other vowels.

Start on E above Middle C. Ascend in semitones as high as is comfortable and then come back down.

You can make up other musical patterns based around this five-note exercise to add variety to your falsetto practice. Sing through Radiohead's *High And Dry* (from their album *The Bends*). It's a great one for linking full voice to falsetto. As you sing the 'high' and 'dry', stretch your arms out wide. Think of the Cinderella dress. It should feel great. Don't reach for the falsetto notes; just let them go naturally into your head as you think down. Stay calm and it should just happen. You could also try singing more on the vowel: 'high' would become 'hah' and 'dry' would become 'drah'.

Finally, when you practice make sure you pace yourself. Don't be too ambitious. Start by selecting a few of the exercises. Remember, different exercises suit different people. Also, some singers prefer singing on the more forward 'ee' and 'oo' vowels, whilst others prefer the open vowel 'ah'. It will be helpful to practice all these exercises in time, but experiment with what feels most comfortable for you and start with those.

Begin by practicing for just five minutes. As you get stronger and understand better what you are doing, you can increase it to ten or fifteen minutes. A practice of this length is absolutely fine for most people. Do thirty minutes maximum. It may not sound much but that is a lot of concentrated singing.

Many singers practice their exercises separately from their repertoire. This can be a good idea, as you won't then end up doing too much singing in one go.

CHAPTER 16 SUMMARY

- Working with singing exercises will not only help you develop your voice, it will give you real awareness of how you should be using it.

- The benefits of working with singing exercises regularly include: improving breath control; strengthening your voice; increasing your range; developing your tone and resonance; gaining understanding and control of your registers; and increasing vocal agility.

- Practicing with singing exercises regularly helps to develop appropriate *muscle memory*.

- Working with singing exercises does not have to result in your singing sounding 'operatic' – you still have choices about resonance, style, phrasing, etc.

SECTION FOUR: AUDITIONING AND PERFORMANCE

The majority of people will buy this book to maximise their own singing pleasure – they are the bathtub Beyonces, the private Pavarottis, the wannabe Whitneys. Some of you, however, may want to take your singing one step further and make the transition from lounge to karaoke bar, or perhaps even local open-mic stages.

But for those who take their singing even more seriously, I include here some practical advice on auditioning techniques and performance.

Chapter 17
Auditioning

If you are serious about auditioning then the first rule is, *be fully prepared*. Whether you happen to be auditioning for a part in a school production, a choir, a dramatic/operatic society, the West End/Broadway, a rock/ pop band or reality TV show, the bottom line is that you need to prepare thoroughly. It is vital that you put yourself across in the best possible light, and give clear glimpses of your true potential.

If you haven't prepared fully, this will almost inevitably become evident in the audition, leaving you and the people for whom you are auditioning feeling frustrated and dissatisfied. In some cases, auditionees turn up still not completely sure which song to sing. Apart from anything else, this gives the impression of a lack of commitment, even if this is not the case. Often it is hard to choose the right song, and you need to make sure it is appropriate (see below), but you *must* have decided on something to sing before you go in. A sensible approach is to thoroughly prepare two or three songs.

Virtually all the material in the Performance chapter (see page 143) is relevant to the auditioning situation. The section on energy is vitally important. I won't go into details here but this information is gold dust for any performer.

When you are in an audition it is particularly important to maintain eye contact with the people you are singing to. Remember, don't just stare into space; you want to communicate with the people when you sing and put across your personality. This doesn't mean you have to 'eyeball' one person all the way through. There is a three-second rule for eye contact; if you look at someone for more than three seconds it can feel a little awkward. Also, if you have a problem looking directly at someone, look between their eyebrows; they honestly won't be able to tell and it may make it feel easier for you. If there are several people in the room, sing to them all. If they don't want to look, or it makes them feel uncomfortable, don't worry, they will look away or probably start writing notes.

A musical director I once worked with told me one of the reasons he employed me for a particular job was that I was the only one auditioning who had looked at and communicated with him.

Among other things, you need to work out how you are going to stand, what you are going to do with your hands, and whether you are going to move around etc. A good tip is to rehearse using a mirror. The aim is to avoid looking too self-conscious. If you do anything odd with your hands, for example, it is this that will pull focus away from you and your singing. If you look relaxed and natural, people will relax into your performance. Rehearse your song or piece, trying out different things and seeing what looks good. Above all you should appear natural and comfortable.

You do not need a full-on dance routine. If dancing is required, singing and dancing auditions are usually separate. If they like what they hear, you will be asked to dance later.

The more prepared you are, the more you will feel in control. Even rehearse walking into the room – remember, you are allowed to smile; in fact, it is highly recommended!

Finally, make sure you look your best – it goes without saying image is very important. Your hair and clothes should complement the musical idiom with which the panel is concerned. Wear clothes you feel comfortable in: avoid clothes that restrict your throat or breathing, and don't, for example, decide to sing in high heels (especially you guys) if you are not used it.

Remember, although image will inevitably enter the equation, it is your voice, personality and (depending on the audition) your acting or dancing ability people are interested in.

Choosing Material

If you are auditioning for a particular part in a musical or opera, your song choice is obviously pretty straightforward. If you are going for a more general audition, say, for a pop band or even a choir you need to have a selection of material. Make a firm decision before you go as to what you are going to sing. Ideally take two songs (or pieces) with you. Decide which is your best and start with that. If they want to hear more, you are then prepared.

You must learn your songs thoroughly. Choose one up-tempo number and a ballad by way of contrast. If you are singing classical music, choose two contrasting pieces, perhaps one in a foreign language.

Depending on the type of audition, you may not get to sing a song the whole way through. The more auditionees there are, the less time you will have to impress the listener. It is therefore a good idea to start with your best song.

Sometimes you will just be asked for a verse and a chorus of one song, but it is always good to have more up your sleeve should you be asked for it. It may be felt, for example, that your first song does not suit your voice or show its full potential.

Choose songs you can sing well, and don't be overambitious. Depending on how experienced a singer you are, it might be an idea to avoid songs with too wide a range – a song that goes too high or low.

It is probably best to steer clear of the most demanding songs associated with virtuoso artists such as Whitney Houston, Christina Aguilera and Stevie Wonder (unless you are also amazing, of course!) as most people can't really do them justice. Also, there is nothing more embarrassing than someone trying to reproduce other people's licks and doing it badly. Believe me, I have heard plenty of this, and it's not pleasant!

You want your individuality and personality to come across. A good tip is to choose a song the panel won't have already heard fifty times that week. At the same time, I wouldn't recommend choosing something *too* quirky or too much outside the mainstream.

If you are singing with an accompanist, be nice to them. If you are not nice, they can give you a tough time! Make sure the piece is not fiendishly difficult – some accompanists are better readers than others. The copy of the score you give the accompanist should be in the right key. If you are singing in a different key to the sheet music, at least ensure the chords of the key in which you wish to sing are clearly written in. Ideally, have a proper chord chart or specially transposed version (music teachers will often do this for you). Sticky-tape the music together in such a way that there aren't any tricky page-turns. This will also help to guard against the music falling off the piano mid-song!

Confession time: Many years ago I was playing the piano for some auditions for a musical. Unbeknown to the auditionees I was also the musical director of the project at the time.

One rather pushy-looking young woman came in with a piece of music I can only describe, from a sight-reading point of view, as a nightmare. Now, I am no Ashkenazy, but I am a pretty good sight-reader. However, I had never seen the like of this piece before. It had numerous changes of time and key. I freely admit I made a bit of a hash of it, but rather than seeing the funny side, the woman insulted me, saying crossly that other pianists had all been able to play it perfectly well before. Needless to say she totally blew her chances of singing another song. I moved swiftly on to the sight-reading, and you can probably guess the kind of piece I chose for her. I'm not normally vindictive in the slightest, but I guess if the story teaches us anything, it is that you should always treat people with respect and good manners – whoever they might be.

Learning The Song

Make sure you know the words inside out, as nerves often make your mind go blank, and if you feel a little unsure there is a chance you will dry up. If you have difficulty remembering lyrics write them out. Learn line one, then lines one and two, then lines one, two and three etc. Often the links between verses cause problems. Giving yourself a mental picture or 'hook' based on the words can help you remember how one verse leads on from another.

Singing along with the original song is the best way to learn the tune accurately. Learn it a line at a time, just as you did with the lyrics. When you know one verse inside out, sing it without the track. You may think you have got it, but when you take the backing away it can be surprisingly difficult. You begin to realise how much your singing is guided and scaffolded by the original.

Many singers learn a song completely straight – singing it with the same phrasing the whole way through. Like the experienced artist, you should aim to vary things a little. Pay close attention to detail – where the melody changes, for example, or where there are variations in verses, in the middle eights, choruses or ad-libs. The idea is not to reproduce an exact copy of the original, particularly if it is too vocally demanding. You should, however, aim to vary your phrasing as this is an indicator of how mature a musician you are.

Music Theatre Singing

Use the same method to learn show music. Obviously the ad-libbing and improvisation elements will not be as relevant. If you play an instrument it can be an advantage, particularly if you are learning the song from the printed sheet music. You may be able to work out the melody. If you don't play an instrument or read music very well, you may know someone who can record it for you. You will be able to find recordings of most pieces online.

There are different things to concentrate on depending upon the type of music you are singing. In music theatre the emphasis may be more on character performance. Certainly you need strong delivery of the words (see the *Interpretation* section, page 149). Pay close attention to the dynamics (louds and softs) marked in the music. Employing dynamic contrast can really bring a song to life. Don't feel you have to 'belt' everything out in order to achieve a strong performance – moments of (quiet) tenderness and beauty are equally as powerful.

Classical Singing

Again, you can use the same method to learn classical repertoire. Be careful if you are singing in a foreign language. Make efforts to get your pronunciation accurate. I used to get foreign-language speakers to record the words for me. I would also back it up by listening to the original wherever possible.

It is essential to have the accompaniment with which to practice. You may have a friend who can play it for you. If not, it will definitely be worth paying a professional accompanist to run through it with you before the audition. Singing with an accompanist or coach is a very different experience to singing at home in your bedroom or lounge. They can help you with dynamics and phrasing, and by working together you will become familiar and 'tied into' the accompaniment.

If you are singing choral music, following the score while singing along with a recording of the piece is invaluable.

Getting Technical

Whatever style of music you are singing, aim to sing well technically. The underlying technique is the same for all kinds of singing, but you have a huge amount of choice as an individual singer; you use your 'ear' to decide and direct the specific sound you want to make.

Here is a checklist of the main areas of technique on which to focus:

- Make sure you have worked out where to breathe.
- Practice the words singing on the vowel.
- Work on where you are resonating the sound.
- Check you are not pushing your chest register too high.
- Try some of the bodywork exercises as you practice e.g. the pot on the head, arm-swinging, fencing etc. (see page 45).

Learn your material thoroughly: the better you rehearse it, the better the performance. You usually find the more you sing a song, the easier it becomes, and then you can concentrate on delivery. The following chapter on performance is relevant to any singer in an audition situation or when singing live.

CHAPTER 17 SUMMARY

- The golden rule for any audition is, BE FULLY PREPARED.

- Look your best, but wear clothes which are comfortable to sing in and which are compatible with the kind of music the audition requires.

- If the choice of material is yours, choose your songs carefully – generally prepare a slow number and a more up-tempo one. Sing your best first.

- Make sure you have a copy of the music for the accompanist in the right key.

- You must know the song inside out – 'over-learn' your material.

- Whichever style of music you are singing, you should aim to sing your piece well technically. Use the checklist above.

Chapter 18
Performance

For many people, performing in public for the first time is a daunting prospect. It can certainly be a nerve-wracking experience, regardless of the occasion – and even the most seasoned performers suffer from nerves. But don't worry, I am going to give you some strategies to help you prepare. In this section I talk about general preparation, projection, song delivery and interpretation. I shall then discuss stage fright and give you some exciting mental visualisation techniques that will help you cope with it as well as improve your overall performance.

As far as I am concerned, live performance is what it is all about. Don't be dispirited if your first efforts are disappointing – singing and performing live gets easier the more you do it. I hope the following advice will allow you to feel more at ease when performing in front of people. The more relaxed and prepared you are, the more you and your audience will enjoy your performance, and the better it is likely to be.

Preparation

As I emphasised in the auditioning section, you need to learn your material really well. I know sometimes, despite all your best intentions, you will just not have had enough time to rehearse thoroughly. But the more you know your stuff the better, as with the nerves of performance it is easy for things to go wrong.

If you look uncertain and nervous when you sing, then the audience will pick up on this. They will end up feeling ill at ease themselves, which in turn prevents them from being able to relax and enjoy the performance.

If you find learning material difficult, use the methods described in the section on *Auditioning* (see page 136).

Projection

When you sing a song you should *project* it to the audience. Projecting means 'throwing' or 'casting' out. Many people imagine you achieve this by pushing the sound out as loudly as possible. However, consider everything I have said about good technique and resonance. You are your instrument. If you push the sound out you will risk losing resonance, support and, in all likelihood, after time, your voice. You need to draw the sound into your body to achieve optimum power and resonance.

Projection is much more than just belting out a song at the top of your voice. It is about putting a song across with feeling and meaning. A performance does not have to be loud for it to be powerful. You want to draw the audience in and move them. The more conviction and emotional intensity you can draw on, the better your performance will be.

Eva Cassidy is a great example of a singer who was able to communicate maximum emotional intensity. Not only did she possess a truly beautiful voice, she also had a rare capacity to engage with an audience in a way that can only be described as spell-binding.

You should project some of your personality to the listener. It is important as a performer to connect with your audience on a personal level.

As you will see later, one of my all-time favourite singers is the amazing jazz singer Kurt Elling. As well as being a wonderful singer he is a natural communicator. He makes it his job to fully engage the audience, allowing them to forget the outside world and just be in the moment with him. He dislikes people videoing any part of his gigs as he believes this destroys the intimacy and connection he has built up with each individual in the audience. He believes the live experience should be properly live.

People are drawn in consciously, but also *unconsciously,* by all kinds of things you do with your body when singing. It could be you maintain strong eye contact with the audience or that, through gesture and expression, you can successfully put across warmth and self-confidence.

Some artists are adept at using hand signals and gestures to communicate; others will capture and hold the attention of their audience by energetically moving around the stage. Some artists stay quite still, but they have such focused energy you just can't help being drawn into their performance. There is no one approach or personality type that will reach out to an audience and engage them.

I would, however, recommend you spend some time closely watching performances of the really big stars. Note what they are doing with their eyes, bodies, arms and hands, especially those things that appear to get a reaction from the audience. Now try building some of these into your own performance, all the time monitoring their effect; you can then retain those elements that appear to produce the desired reaction.

When you are performing, focus is crucially important. If you are unfocused the audience will quickly lose interest in you. They need to totally *believe* in you. If you lack focus, you will lack authority. This is a key part of projection.

I went to a gig recently where, in between songs, the singer picked up her water bottle. She did it in such a self-conscious, almost apologetic way, that this simple act became a distraction which destroyed the 'spell' of her performance. Whatever you do you must do with focus and energy.

What you do with your eyes is very important. Eye contact is the most basic form of communication. If you look at the audience it is difficult for them not to respond to you.

However hard they try, some people still find maintaining eye contact with their audience incredibly difficult. If you are one of these people, try focusing between the eyebrows of individual members of the audience. This is much better than just staring into space, or, worse still, at your feet. You will still get the response from the audience you want without having to look them straight in the eyes.

Whatever the size of venue you happen to be singing in, remember you need to sing to people at the back as well as the front (and, depending on the venue, in the direction of the upper circle!).

Watching a singer who is just staring out into the distance switches me off as a listener. The unconscious exchange runs something like: if they're not bothered about looking at me, I can't be bothered to listen to them.

Not being able to achieve eye contact with an audience may also suggest a lack of confidence and, again, if you feel the singer is nervy, you will not in turn be relaxed as a listener. Most of us need adrenalin to ensure we give our best performance, and facing the audience is part of what gets it flowing. Those artists who communicate strongly with their audience give the most powerful performances, period.

So, projection involves a number of things, but remember, you don't have to push your voice to unreasonable limits in order to achieve it.

Personal Energy

Energy in performance is key. When you perform you need to have a high level of focused personal energy to engage the listener. This goes for when you are recording vocals as well as live. It is useful to imagine a 'scale' of personal energy ranging from 1 to 10 where 1 is very low energy and 10 is very high. Using this scale, when you perform you need to be 8, 9 or 10.

There are various ways you can think of the energy. You can link it to the breath using the in-breath to raise your energy up. Imagine the more deeply and slowly you draw the breath into your lungs the more your energy rises. A good way to practice this is with the three-part breathing on page 18. Think of the breath flowing in at different energy levels. Play around with this.

I imagine a thermometer stretching from my tummy button to my sternum. If I am energy level 1 the red line of the thermometer stays at the bottom and as my energy rises so does the red line, until it has risen to my sternum taking me to energy level 10.

The clock face is a real favourite. Stand with your arms straight down by your sides. This is 1 o'clock. Gradually take your arms up above your head. Half way is 5 o'clock and when you've reached the top you're at 10 o'clock. Practice breathing into 1 o'clock, energy 1, and then walk round the room at energy level 1. Then raise your arms to 5 o'clock, energy level 5, and walk around at energy 5. Now take your arms all the way up over your head to 10 o'clock, energy 10. Walk around at energy 10.

Lots of performers I know use this to get them into the right zone before they go on stage. A TV presenter I worked with who had lost confidence uses this before she does pieces to camera, and it works a treat. Not only can you use it to prepare for going on stage, but also walking into an audition or even an interview – it is powerful stuff.

Energy is contagious. If you have a high level of focused energy people will feel it. Conversely, if you have low energy people will feel that and they will switch off from you. Also there are certain things that may happen that will make you suddenly lose your energy.

We all know those times when things aren't going too well – say, for example, the sound is awful or you forget a lyric. In that moment your energy can plummet from 8 to 1. When your energy goes you will find it hard to keep the singing going. You will lose your emotional connection and it can be hard to recover. However, if you recognise that it is your energy that has been affected, by thinking about it (if you have practiced) you can push your energy back up. It's incredible what a difference this makes.

The unsympathetic listener can be a killer – you know, the person in the front row looking completely bored. Never focus on them. I know it's human nature to want to please everyone but we never can. We have no idea what their story might be. Maybe they're feeling ill, or their cat got run over that morning, we just don't know. They have the ability to completely suck the energy out of you if you let them. Even if there are ninety-nine smiling faces we will almost inevitably focus on the one with a face like thunder. You need to learn to ignore these individuals and get on with your own performance, keeping your energy level high. Furthermore, if they are nasty enough to be trying to put you off, and this is incredibly rare, don't give them the pleasure of succeeding.

You can learn a lot more about the use of personal energy in *Communicate With Charisma* by Tom Bruno-Magdich and Jo Thompson.

Song Delivery

You need energy, focus, commitment and emotion to put across a song well: take Mick Jagger and Andrea Bocelli – two very different singers, yet similar in that they both possess all these attributes in abundance. Although the style of music they sing is clearly dissimilar, both singers have real charisma and a powerful stage presence, causing you to be drawn into their performance.

Obviously, being on top of your technique when you sing will make the singing a lot more reliable and polished. However, having a perfect technique, many of you will be delighted to hear, is not the be all and end all. Some great artists have not got the best voices but their delivery of a song is very powerful.

Words

Chord structure, melody and instrumentation are at the heart of the mood or emotion of any song or piece of music. The lyrics also have a major part to play.

Regardless of the style of music, you really have to *mean* (or at least look/ sound like you mean) the words of a song to put them across convincingly. The listener should be left with a strong impression of the meaning of the song and be moved in some way – left feeling optimistic, happy, sad or thoughtful etc. If you have an emotional 'thought' when you sing (happy, sad, angry etc.), this will come across in your singing and 'speak' to the listener. It will give your performance an attitude or emotional edge.

Stylistically, in classical and show music, the words are more pronounced than in jazz and rock & pop, and there is a greater emphasis on the consonants. D's and t's and other word endings, for example, are generally 'harder' and more deliberate.

In music theatre, particularly, the singer's diction needs to be clear, as the form obviously involves the telling of a story or drama. In jazz and rock & pop, the delivery of the words is traditionally more laid-back and conversational. However you pronounce the words, remember the emphasis should always be on the vowel, to ensure optimum resonance.

If you have a song that requires you to fit a lot of words into a short space, try taking the pressure off the front of your mouth. If you strive to force the words out, your tongue will get stuck and you will trip over them.

Imagine that rather than spitting the words out with your lips, teeth and tongue, you say them with a lightness. Alternatively you can articulate them further back in your mouth. Your tongue should feely springy and light and your lips should just gently touch when they need to. It is almost as if the words are running towards your mouth, jumping in and springing into the back.

Fast rappers are great exponents of this. Check out Busta Rhymes' verse on Chris Brown's *Look at Me Now*. The speed of it is mind-blowing.

People who have problems pronouncing their 'r's (sounding like 'w's) will need to articulate more with their tongues. The 'w' sound is made by the mouth shape being slightly too round.

American Accent

A great deal of popular music is sung with an American accent. This is because much of it has its roots in the American blues. Some songs just don't quite sound right or 'authentic' without Americanisms. It can be overdone, of course – English-sounding 'me's' and 'my's', for example, can just sound too straight (too 'Julie Andrews', if you know what I mean). Recording your efforts and listening back to them is a good way to check you sound 'authentic' rather than phoney and corny.

Having said this, there are plenty of highly successful artists and bands who have a definite (British) regional sound – think of Coldplay, Radiohead, Lily Allen and The Arctic Monkeys etc., and to suggest 'Americanising' the way they sing would be ridiculous and to miss the point.

Interpretation

Everyone has heard the phrase 'making a song your own', well this is what interpretation is all about. It means taking a song and putting your own personal mark on it. There are many things to consider when working on interpretation: technique, words, phrasing, improvisation, emotion, intensity, energy and focus. I have given you a lot of information about all of these, so it is up to you to put this knowledge into practice.

It may be that you are singing a classical aria that demands beautiful line and tone, or a song from a show that requires plenty of character. You may be singing an improvisatory jazz piece or a sustained up-tempo rock & pop song. All of these demand different skills and qualities, or more accurately a combination of many similar things.

1. Try singing your song with an emotional 'thought' – think happy, sad, angry, vulnerable, and see what difference it makes.

2. Practice emphasising the *meaning* of the words.

3. Work on your phrasing: singing behind the beat, on the beat, ahead of the beat.

4. Try to improvise around the melody. Don't be overambitious; small excursions from the tune are fine for starters.

The Band Vocalist

Everything I have said about performance is relevant whether you are a soloist or a band member. If you are gigging there are, however, some other considerations.

There is no doubt that stepping out on to a stage for the first time in front of an audience – regardless of how well rehearsed you are – can be a nerve-wracking occasion. It is true to say that the more you do it, the better it gets, but there are a number of things you can work on to help you prepare yourself better and build your confidence.

Firstly, learn your material thoroughly. Make sure all your songs are really well 'sung in'. Generally speaking, the more you have sung a song, the easier it becomes and the less likely you are to strain your voice.

It is a good idea to 'over-learn' your songs. When you are on stage and actually facing an audience you may freeze. The words are usually the first to go and that can be very scary, so you want them to be almost second nature. The more familiar you are with your material the better. You will be able to relax more easily knowing it is firmly lodged in your memory banks, and this will make you feel freer to improvise.

If you are doing a gig or showcase, make sure you know your running order – there is nothing worse than an embarrassing pause while everyone gets their act together.

Learning to perform on stage takes practice. Obviously, some people are naturals and feel totally at home on stage, but most of us have to work at it. Initially, moving around the stage can feel awkward. If you feel you are a natural 'mover' then great, but if you feel uncomfortable you will look uncomfortable and the audience will share your discomfort. Holding a microphone helps, as you then have something to do with your hands. Avoid, however, the habitual curling and uncurling of fingers around the mic as you sing. I see an increasing number of people doing this, especially on shows such as *The X Factor*. My view is that it comes across as an annoying affectation which detracts from the singing.

Some singers feel more comfortable using a mic stand as it literally (and psychologically) gives them something more to hold on to. Percussion instruments such as tambourines or shakers can also be useful props.

The instrumental breaks can be tricky; you need to keep your focus here. If you are not the kind of singer who enjoys leaping around, you above all need to look like you are well *into* the music. Look at the audience and keep eye contact (I think this is the most powerful technique). It can work well just standing still and listening to the band. Some singers prefer to look down; others even turn their backs to the audience. It is up to you and what you are comfortable with. Whatever you do, you must carry it out with conviction, but make sure you have practiced it first; don't leave it until your first gig to try something out.

It can be easier on stage if you have an instrument to 'hide' behind, but this doesn't mean your performance should be lazy.

One of the things that frightens so many people, often more than the singing itself, is interacting with the audience at the start of a gig and in between numbers. Many avoid doing any work on it, simply because they feel embarrassed or self-conscious.

If you are the lead vocalist, invariably it will be your job to provide links. Script these; rehearse some key comments, but never do jokes unless you can deliver them confidently. Many singers don't say much at all – just introducing a few of their songs, leaving their music to do the talking. Don't rely on being able to come up with something brilliant on the spot. Preparing some key scripts in advance, of course, does not preclude additional improvised efforts; it just provides a skeleton structure or safety net. Interacting with the audience is a vital part of your performance and should not be overlooked.

Watch people who are good at working an audience and analyse what they are doing. A lot of what sounds spontaneous will, in fact, be rehearsed – you will know this if you have seen certain shows more than once. Try not to be too ambitious in the early stages of your career; keep it fairly simple initially. In time working with an audience will come more naturally.

Try not to get too carried away in the excitement of the performance. I have heard of guitarists suffering cut fingers and tambourine players bruising their thighs! More seriously, though, if you lose your focus you can end up pushing your voice too far and doing some damage – ranging from a small swelling of the cords to (if repeated regularly) the formation of nodules and other more serious vocal injuries.

Always remember to warm up, either by using exercises, or at least some gentle singing. Everyone is different, and some voices warm up more slowly than others, but try to do about ten minutes. Don't do too much and tire out your voice before you've even started. Make sure you warm up before a sound check. Don't start your performance 'cold' – you won't sound as good, and you stand more chance of harming your voice. I shall be going through warm-ups in some detail later (see page 188).

If you can't hear yourself on stage, don't push it, there is no point. The chances are no one else will be able to hear you either – even if you are screaming at the top of your voice. Unfortunately, not all sound systems are very good. With any luck your monitors will be loud enough, but quite often you will feel you are fighting a losing battle.

Trying to get the band to turn down a notch is usually pretty difficult. Stand your ground – even turning down a little can really help. Make them see if the band loses its singer due to voice problems they are going nowhere.

Some people find earplugs help. For those with more cash, 'in ears' are the business. You will have seen singers on TV wearing these discreet earphones, molded to the shape of their individual ears. They allow you to hear your own voice properly, along with a mix of the track or band, making it easier to avoid forcing your voice against the track, which in turn will help with pitching. In ears take a while to get used to, so make sure you have rehearsed well with them before performing live. A word of warning: some singers have themselves turned up so loud in the mix that they sing way out of tune!

Gigging Sound

Those of us who have done a lot of gigs will have experienced the horrors of terrible sound equipment, and sometimes equally terrible sound engineers. If you end up struggling to overcome some kind of giant acoustic octopus while you are trying to sing, it can certainly take away the pleasure. If you have a good sound balance on stage it makes a massive difference. I include here some information about equipment and on-stage sound which you may find helpful, as well as a few tips to get things running smoothly.

Monitor speakers allow each person on stage to have their own personal mix. For example, the singer might have very loud vocals, including a good blend of backing vocals, a bit of guitar, a fair amount of keyboards (as they have no acoustic level) plus a small amount of bass.

There are also side-fill speakers that are designed to give a complete mix of the on-stage sound to suit the band. These speakers are very important because they allow you to move away from your monitor and enjoy more freedom on stage.

Always try to strike up a rapport with the person in charge of the sound. You may not be able to hear yourself as well as the rest of the band. A few friendly words early on will encourage the sound person to be more attentive to your changing needs during the gig. If you don't hit it off, it can sometimes be a nightmare.

All vocalists want to be heard above the band (and quite rightly), but appreciate that it is difficult to get the drums below a certain level. Yes, I know, they are always too loud.

To avoid the impression I have it in for drummers exclusively, I would add it also helps if you don't have the guitar stack pointing directly at your ear.

Singers invariably have no reverb in their monitors as reverb goes back into the mic and makes the sound muddy; so don't give the monitor engineer a hard time if you were expecting it.

Stage Fright

Relaxation is a powerful tool in combating stage fright. As I have mentioned previously, apart from their other uses, breathing exercises have a calming effect. They can help stop your breathing and your body from going into panic mode.

Giving yourself time to lie on the floor and focus on your breath (see *Breathing Exercises,* page 17) will help you overcome any feelings of panic. It is important to make the point, however, that pre-show nerves are not necessarily a bad thing, as most of us need a certain amount of adrenalin to pull off a good performance.

Incidentally, if you suffer badly from nerves, a few stiff drinks before you go on is not really the answer. Although alcohol may well make you feel a bit more relaxed, your vocals can suffer. Alcohol increases the blood supply to your vocal cords, causing them to swell. As a result, the sound you produce will not be as reliable as usual.

One singer I worked with studied method acting to help her deal with stage fright. She was able to switch off her fear by visualising herself in non-threatening situations, for example, scrubbing her back in the bath or lying on a beach. It worked well for her, particularly in slow numbers, but it wouldn't work for everyone – if overdone there is a danger of 'drifting off' and losing connection with your audience.

Visualisation

As we have already seen, mental imagery is used a great deal when singing. Sometimes, simply by visualising something (like when we direct the sound into different resonating places), it will happen. Visualisation techniques can also be used to give you a more positive attitude towards your performance.

To give the best vocal performance you need to be practically, physically and mentally prepared. Many performers like to have a quiet period before going on stage in which to relax, rid themselves of nerves, and focus their minds and energy.

Many performers use some form of **positive imaging** (like that employed by top sports stars) to get themselves into the optimum frame of mind before performing and to trigger key muscle memory. Finding the right environment in which to do this can often prove difficult, especially given cramped venues and limited backstage areas, but it is definitely worth trying.

There are many different **positive visualisation** techniques, but here is a simple and effective one for you to try.

Find a quiet place, close your eyes, and relax. Listen to your breathing. Concentrate on the out-breath (this is the relaxing part of breathing).

Visualise yourself singing a particular song from start to finish really well – your best possible performance. You could use a memory of a particular occasion when you were singing at the top of your game, but it doesn't have to be – it could just be the 'idea'. Focus your mind on what you look like and what you are doing with your body.

Next, using the same image or 'film' of yourself, listen to how you sound when you are singing brilliantly like this. Go through the whole song again with this thought in your mind.

Now go through it once more, concentrating on what it feels like – emotionally as well as physically and technically.

The important thing to remember is to go over the song mentally three times, focusing in turn on the visual, auditory and kinaesthetic (feeling) modes. Don't miss one out; the technique is just not as powerful if you do.

What you are creating here is known as a *rehearsed positive state*. It is an exceptionally powerful tool and can make a big difference to how you think of yourself as a performer and consequently how well you are able to perform. It is an empowering technique that deeply reinforces the feeling and belief that you can sing really well. When you perform for real you can draw on these positive thoughts and feelings, enabling you to maximise your performance.

In order to help with this process you can employ what are known as *mental anchors*. As you mentally rehearse the song, for example, you can associate the feelings and thoughts arising from successfully navigating a particularly difficult part of your vocal with the touching of a specific part of your body. Then when you come to sing, simply by touching that body part, the same positive visualisation is *triggered*.

For example, while you are positively visualising how you are sounding at a certain point, you can touch the top of your left thigh with the fingers of your left hand. When you are singing, you touch yourself in the same place and that 'memory' or positive state is triggered.

Visualisation can be extremely useful before any performance, but you can build it into your general practice.

A Cappella Performance

Often in auditions you are required to sing without any accompaniment, but it is not just for auditions that you may have to sing unaccompanied or *a cappella*. Unaccompanied singing has a long and varied history. Moreover, there are many contemporary artists and groups who include *a cappella* songs in their sets, or indeed only ever sing unaccompanied – like the barbershop quartets and choirs.

I love singing in harmony: there is nothing quite like it. I used to sing in a close-harmony jazz group. It was purely for fun, but we sang wonderful arrangements penned by the inspirational and hugely talented jazz pianist, and teacher, Pete Churchill. Pete's love of music and his enthusiasm are infectious. I learned so much about group singing, phrasing, dynamics and improvisation in these sessions. What I learned has stayed with me and has become part of my everyday teaching. Thanks, Pete!

Singing together well is a real discipline. Some absolute masters are the American a cappella Gospel sextet, Take 6. If you haven't heard them it's time you treated yourself. All the members are highly trained musicians and they use their voices as musical instruments. Indeed, they provide their own 'instrumental' backing with their voices. Their arrangements and harmonies are so inventive and they sing together as a wondrously tight unit. The balance of their voices is perfect and their phrasing remarkable. One of my favourite tracks is *Get Away Jordan* from their eponymous debut album *Take 6*.

I have worked with a number of pop bands over the years, helping them to prepare *a cappella* snippets for TV and radio appearances. This is always a popular requirement – the main idea, I guess, being that it shows they really can sing! Often they will do an arrangement of a small part of their latest single, or one of their hits, maybe only singing the chorus. They generally keep it short and sweet, although sometimes they may want something more adventurous.

I have had the great fun and pleasure of working with The Overtones over several years. They regularly sing a cappella, particularly if they're doing a radio or TV interview. Often we will only have two or three hours between us to come up with an arrangement to which everyone contributes. They are all excellent singers and have a real range of voices that blend beautifully. Because they have sung together for such a long time, the way they sing – their style, dynamics and phrasing – has become almost second nature.

I have a specific approach when working with a group. Firstly, I make sure everyone knows their line or harmony. Then we work on these until each member is singing them well. We then move on to group dynamics – getting the louds and softs in the same place. Next I concentrate on phrasing, making sure they are all singing the same length phrases with the same emphasis. Finally, I focus attention on the words and vowel sounds.

The beginnings and ends of phrases need to be tight otherwise the singing will sound sloppy. Ragged 't's and 'd's sound awful. If endings are proving tricky, I give one of the singers the responsibility for sounding them (with the others just 'ghosting').

Getting them to listen closely to each other is vital. They must not just grimly hold on to their line and shut out everyone else. Learning to hear their line as part of the whole is crucial, otherwise the tuning and phrasing will never be good enough. Looking at each other while rehearsing works well (until, as often happens, they all start laughing).

I usually appoint one band member as MD (musical director). Sometimes this doesn't go down very well. You have to be aware of egos as to some this looks or feels like favouritism (fame affects some people in funny ways you know – but my lips are sealed!).

The MD will be responsible for giving starting notes, counting in, and generally keeping the whole thing together. They can achieve this by using a combination of eye contact, gentle conducting, or a slight head gesture.

CHAPTER 18 SUMMARY

- When singing live you need to learn to *project*, or in other words, put a song across with feeling and meaning.

- The audience is drawn in at an unconscious level by all kinds of things you do with your body.

- It is particularly important to achieve eye contact with your audience.

- Maintaining a high level of personal energy is vital when singing live or recording vocals.

- Regardless of the style of music, you have to really *mean* the words of a song to put it across convincingly.

- The clarity of a singer's diction is relatively more important in opera or show music than it is in jazz or rock & pop, chiefly because these forms involve the telling of a clear story or drama.

- It is much easier to sing very wordy songs and fast raps if you lighten off the articulation or place it further back in your mouth.

- Interpretation involves taking a song and putting your own personal mark on it.

- There are many things to consider when working on interpretation: technique, words, phrasing, improvisation, emotion, intensity, sensitivity, energy, focus, etc.

- Band vocalists should always rehearse fully, be clear about running orders, practice their stagecraft and links, strike up a rapport with the sound engineer, warm up properly, and look after their voices.

- Breathing exercises and visualisation techniques can help to relax and prepare a singer before a performance.

- A systematic approach to group harmony singing is suggested in this chapter.

Chapter 19
Recording And Studio Work

Singing in a studio is a very different experience to singing live. Recording vocals well is something I feel passionate about. The singing on some recordings is, to my ears, not as good as it could be. From a professional point of view I find this very frustrating. There are many producers who get good vocals out of their artists, but there are many more who don't. One of my specialist areas is working in studios with singers, helping them to record their tracks – something I love doing.

As far as I am concerned, getting a great performance is what it is all about. Don't be dispirited if your first efforts are disappointing.

Recording Vocals

There are many different ways to go about recording vocals. Obviously much of it is determined by the equipment, resources and time available to you.

What I like to hear in a good vocal are good tuning, great phrasing and feel, emotion, character, energy and an attractive tone. In other words, all the elements that combine to make a great live performance.

Some singers prefer to sing the whole song all the way through; others prefer to record it in sections. My personal preference is a mixture of the two. I like to start with the singer running the song a couple of times to get a good 'vibe' going. Then I like to break it up into sections: record the verse and bridge, then the second verse and bridge. Sometimes we'll just do the verses, then the bridges. It really depends on how vocally demanding the song is. Then I may do the middle eight, followed by the choruses, harmonies and ad-libs.

Often the chorus will be higher than the rest of the song. Consequently, if you do a number of takes it can become tiring quite quickly. This is why I recommend you get the bulk of the singing done first.

Nothing, however, is set in stone. Some singers prefer to record the song 'live' as they find they get a better feel. They will do several takes all the way through and choose the best one. Many singers find it difficult to make a song consistently good all the way through. Even if you record in sections, you may find that you will go back and rework the beginning. The more you work on a song, the more ideas you get.

Many producers 'track' vocals, which means the singer repeats exactly what they have sung over again. These two 'tracks' will then be played simultaneously and, of course, this thickens up the vocal sound. On backing vocals and harmonies especially, three or more tracks are sometimes added.

Often, to add depth to the sound, the lead line is added (quietly) an octave lower. Whispers are also used to add texture. This is where the singer delivers the words in time with the track, but with a whispered sound.

For a final word on the recording of vocals I turn to my long-time friend and Grammy-winning producer, Kipper.

"I have the good fortune to have produced some of my favourite singers of all time – James Taylor, Mary J Blige, Shawn Colvin and, of course, Sting, to name just four! Singers of this calibre I believe are largely born not bred, however, they too need to employ focus, discipline and technique in order to maximise their potential.

As a producer my role is to get a great sound for these performers to work with, create a suitable atmosphere and ambience which is relaxed and conducive to the song, and to be a positive sounding board able to offer ideas or advice when needed.

I always like to have the singer in the control room with me when recording lead vocals. This enables me to have a more intense working relationship with the artist and the song, whilst removing the clinical 'studio' vibe that a vocal booth and glass wall can create.

Some handy tips:

Record and keep absolutely everything you sing or play; one never knows when an inspirational moment may arrive.

If you are having tuning problems, remove one side of the headphones to reference your voice through the air. You may find there is too much reverb on your voice or that your vocal balance is wrong.

Never feel that 'this is the one'. Each take is work in progress, and all the details you may obsess over today may have evaporated tomorrow. Simply enjoy the song and be in the moment.

In The Vocal Booth

You need to look after your voice when you are recording. Make sure you warm up properly beforehand – not too much, though, as you will probably have a lot of singing to do. Drink lots of water and take rests when you feel you need to. You can do the straw exercise to help you relax your voice. Don't let the producer bully you into singing if your voice feels really tired as you risk damaging it. Don't let people smoke around you.

Some producers (like Kipper and another old friend, Fraser T Smith) have a real flair for recording vocals and getting the best out of the singer. Unfortunately, there are others who, when it comes to working with singers, don't really know what they are doing. Some may have done a bit of singing themselves, or had the odd singing lesson. I find it irritating, though, when they try to make out they are an authority on singing and vocals when patently they are not. These people can often confuse a singer (a little bit of knowledge being a dangerous thing) by trying to push them to do something technically inappropriate.

One singer I know told me the producer she was working with got her to hold an amp against her tummy to help her to support her voice. I have rarely heard anything so ridiculous. It could only help her strain her voice due to the effort of holding it. And how that's supposed to get you in the right relaxed state for delivering a great vocal is beyond me.

We are all different and, when it comes to singing, it is most definitely not the case that 'one size fits all'. What works for one singer may well not work for another. Many producers will try to push a singer to their limit by demanding they sing material much too high for their voice, or by expecting them to keep going even when their voice is showing clear signs of fatigue or strain. They may, as I mentioned, insist the singer tries something alien and technically inappropriate or unhelpful.

It is true that you need to make yourself work hard, and that studio time can be very expensive, but that doesn't mean you have to strain your voice and risk temporary or even permanent damage. If someone asks you to do something that is continually uncomfortable vocally, stand up for yourself and simply refuse to do it.

Note: Never use any vocal sprays or chemical remedies to get you through a vocal. If your voice has packed up there is a good reason for it. Using these things in order to continue singing is akin to applying a painkilling spray to an athlete's torn or damaged muscle and expecting them to carry on competing – not recommended!

Backing Vocals And Harmonies

Many songs do not sound complete without the addition of backing vocals. Good BVs enhance and often totally transform a song by adding depth, colour and excitement. On recordings, the solo artist will often sing their own BVs, or they will be sung by other band members or professional backing/session singers.

Backing singing is an art in itself. The top session singers, it goes without saying, have all got very good, reliable voices and are excellent performers generally. They really know their stuff and have worked hard at it over the years. They will have listened to a great amount and variety of music, paying particular attention to style and phrasing, and will have copied and practiced the best examples.

However, not everyone has to be the most amazing singer to do BVs. Many instrumentalists in bands have to sing them, and indeed it is a real asset for a musician to be able to sing strong BVs – there is no doubt you are a more attractive proposition to bands and agencies if you can. Interestingly, a lot of instrumentalists come to me for help with their backing singing. Some end up discovering voices they never thought they had, and some, as a result, even move on to singing lead vocals.

Backing vocals can be used in many different ways. On recorded tracks there would usually be more BVs than live. However, if someone is singing along to a backing track, most of the BVs will be on it (often the lead is also there, but just reduced in volume). When singing live with a band, pre-recorded BV tracks are sometimes used and would be triggered by one of the instrumentalists.

Backing vocals are often used to enhance a lead line – tracking it, as I have already mentioned, or singing it an octave higher or lower. Harmonising the lead in 2, 3 or 4 parts is common. You wouldn't want to do it all the way through a song, but in the right places it can sound great. Sometimes just harmonising the last one or two words of a phrase can be very effective.

Some people have a natural ability to be able to pick out a harmony line effortlessly. Most singers have the capability but it just takes practice. BVs can be simple or complex, depending on the music, but here are a few suggestions by way of a starting point for developing your BVs.

If you are singing in two parts, the easiest harmony to take is a 3rd above the lead line. So, for example, if the melody started on a C you would start on the E above. You would then move in exactly the same way as the lead.

Another simple line would be a 6th below. This would mean if the lead were on a C you would start on the E below, and then move with the melody.

When singing a three-part harmony, base it around a triad (the first, third and fifth notes of the chord you are playing). Don't always sing this in root position; you can invert it (turn it around). For example, you could have the 3rd at the bottom, then the 5th, and then the root (or the first note of the scale) on top.

You won't always be moving with the melody, or singing the words. Backing vocals can be used more as a textural filler and are often structured around instrumental ideas found in a song – maybe a guitar or keyboard riff. These would usually be sung on oo's, ah's and hums, but they still follow the harmonic patterns. I love 'scrunchy' harmonies and, naturally, there are many variations more complicated than the ones mentioned above. However, I am trying to keep it pretty straightforward; all the harmonies I have mentioned are based around the movement of the chords.

Don't overdo the BVs to the extent that things sound too cluttered. Usually the lead singer will sing at least one verse on their own. The backing may then come in for the second verse or the chorus. In a chorus you may want to emphasise certain words, making the backing more chant-like. It may answer the lead line. In some songs the backing takes over and forms the 'hook' of the song; the lead singer is then free to improvise over the top. Many songs end in this way.

Some people find sticking to a harmony line difficult, but it just takes practice. There are a few things you can try that might help. First, as you listen to songs, try picking out the backing and join in with it. Next, take a simple tune. Record yourself singing it and try to work out a simple harmony – maybe a 3rd above – and keep singing along with yourself. The more confident you get, the more ambitious you will become.

How you sing the backing vocals is very important. It is no good if you have all the theory but consistently sing out of tune or very weakly. You need to work on your technique. It is important to have confidence in your own singing and to know how to avoid 'pushing' your voice too hard.

Instrumentalists who have reasonably high voices often complain to me that they are forever being asked to take the high harmony. They find this all right in the studio, but once they are gigging their voices are shot after a few numbers. My best tip is for men to sing in *falsetto* or *head voice,* and for women to sing in *head voice* or *mixed register.* Many people are reluctant to try this at first, but when they do, they soon discover how it protects their voice and, with practice, they can get it to sound strong. (Remember, always 'think down' as you go up and forward in your head!)

Make sure that BVs are well rehearsed; it makes such a difference when they are tight. Ensure you have all decided exactly where you are beginning and ending notes, where you are getting louder or softer, and what vowel sounds you are using. Make sure no individual's voice is sticking out: it is important for the sound to be a reasonable blend. Practice without any accompaniment so that you can really hear each other. It is surprising how many people have never thought of doing this.

Whether preparing BVs for live gigs or recordings, they are well worth spending time on since they can make all the difference to a song.

Mic Technique

People often imagine there is some great secret to mastering the use of a mic. In fact, there is very little to learn, and most of it is common sense. Using a mic properly is something you can master very quickly.

Most importantly, you need to know how to produce an even sound, so if you are singing high or low, the volume should be consistent. This is achieved by moving into the mic for softer and lower notes, and away from the mic for louder or higher notes. If you are using a hand-held mic, you move the mic itself. Don't overdo this. Some people develop a habit of pulling the mic away much too far and the sound disappears altogether or comes and goes in waves.

Hold the mic in front of your mouth, not so close that your lips are touching it, but near enough for the sound to be picked up. It is important to stay 'on the mic' because if you move too far away not only will your voice be quieter it will lose a lot of its presence.

You need to mind your 'p's and 'd's because they can 'pop' on the mic. Also, in order to avoid sibilance (hissing 's' sounds), rather than singing directly into it on some phrases, you can move *across* the mic. Be careful, however, not to overdo this as your voice will get lost in the mix. As is the case with all aspects of mic technique, this will quickly become second nature with practice.

Most singers like to have reverb added to the sound. Reverb electronically creates an ambience for the dry signal. It can be set to give the impression of singing anywhere, from a small bathroom to a huge concert hall. It is much harder singing with a dry sound.

If you have tried singing in a small or cluttered room, and then compared this to singing in a church or a big empty hall, you can't help noticing a huge difference. In the former environment the sound is absorbed by furniture, curtains etc. In a large hall or even in an empty room, the sound is free to ring around and resonate. Singing automatically feels easier. If you haven't experienced this before, next time you come across a room which has been cleared for decorating, have a good sing!

A word of caution. It is not good practice to only sing with a mic as you will never establish a good vocal technique this way. It will prevent you from developing support, resonance, sustain, and evenness of tone amongst other things.

Someone came to me after being taught by a well-known teacher of rock & pop singers. In her lessons she had only ever sung pop songs using a mic. Having had lessons for three years with this person, she had developed no awareness of resonance, openness, body use, support or breath control. I find this almost unbelievable: sure it's a good idea to rehearse with a mic if you are going to perform, but not all the time.

Lip-Synching

Some singers, when miming, hold the mic really close to their mouths to cover up poor lip-synching. Certainly, lip-synching can be tricky to get tight if you have a lot of words to deliver. For lip-synching to look good you have to work at it. Practice by watching yourself in a mirror along with the track. Actually singing the song will help to make your lip-synching accurate and convincing.

People do put an importance on good lip-synching. I have actually been employed to work on some films and videos to ensure that the lip-synching looks authentic.

Sight Singing

Sight singing is the ability to sing music from a printed score without having previously rehearsed it. You do not need to read music or sight sing to be a great singer – many professional singers do neither and will never need to learn. However, being able to read music has many advantages, and having the ability to sight-sing can make life a lot easier. In addition, it will mean you are more desirable for certain singing jobs.

In order to sight-sing, you first need to be able to read music. Clearly, reading music is not something you pick up overnight and it takes plenty of practice. Those who have played an instrument from an early age normally have an advantage since they will usually have studied written music. If you are going to sing in a choir or have ambitions to be a session singer, there are obvious advantages to sharpening up your reading.

Classical musicians tend to be the best readers as they will generally have studied score-written music for many years, depending on how long they have been playing. A great number of musicians, particularly in the rock & pop field, don't read a note of music. This is true of many of the best instrumentalists and vocalists I have known. These people have incredibly well developed 'ears' and have never had to read a note. For many, it feels like trying to join a club to which you don't really belong, and never will.

Understandably, if you play brilliantly by ear already, it might seem pointless to start learning notation from scratch. 'Is it worth it?' I hear you ask.

Well, learning to read music has many advantages. If you are singing with a choir and following scores, it is obviously a huge help.

For those musicians aspiring to professional status, the more skilled you are the better. As a professional singer, you may limit your options of your work if you can't read. Certainly, much studio work is done by ear, but sometimes there will be a score to read. Turning up for a session and finding a score on the music stand can be a wobbly moment for a non-reader.

Musical notation is actually very logical and, although it does take time to learn to read, it really is not all that difficult. There are many books around on music theory and sight singing which are written in user-friendly language. I will limit myself here to a few useful tips.

In order to sight-sing you need to be familiar with and be able to sing the intervals on the stave – or, in other words, combine what you see on the page with what you hear in your head. An interval is the 'distance' between one note and the next. The interval between A and C, for example, is a third (ABC); between A and E is a fifth (ABCDE); between A and G is a seventh (ABCDEFG), and so on.

Something that has helped a lot of people fix the intervals in their head is to link them to a song they know well. Let me explain. You can use the first two notes of a familiar song as an anchor. For example, the song *Yesterday* (by The Beatles) starts with a major 2nd; *Summertime* starts with a major 3rd; *Auld Lang Syne* is a 4th; *Scarborough Fair* is a (perfect) 5th; *My Way* is a major 6th; *Somewhere* (from *West Side Story*) is a minor 7th; *Over The Rainbow* is an octave. You need to learn to combine what these intervals look like on the stave with what they sound like, so that the pattern is instantly recognisable.

When reading music always think in terms of patterns and shapes, especially when you are looking at a piece for the first time. You need to learn the notes both visually and aurally.

It is more difficult to learn to read if you don't play an instrument, as you will have nothing to use as a point of reference. For this reason, if you are serious about learning to sight-read, I would recommend you buy a keyboard.

You also need to practice reading rhythm and, again, there are many good tutor books that work around tapping simple rhythms, gradually increasing their difficulty. You can also use songbooks or scores alongside the appropriate recording. Study the music and follow it while listening to the track. There are books and online resources that have all the band parts transcribed. These are brilliant to work with, as you can follow each part in turn.

Following recordings of choral works, symphonies and concertos with their scores is ideal. Start with the simpler works of classical music composers such as Mozart, Haydn or Beethoven; they shouldn't be too hard to follow.

CHAPTER 19 SUMMARY

- When recording vocals you should try to achieve good tuning, great phrasing and feel, emotion, character, energy, and a great tone.

- Most producers 'track' vocals, which means the singer repeats exactly what they have sung over again in order to thicken up the vocal sound.

- To add depth and texture to the sound, the words are often whispered in time with the lead line, or the melody is sung an octave lower.

- It is important for singers to look after themselves in the vocal booth by warming up properly and applying good basic voice care.

- Backing singing is an art in itself, but there are some general approaches and skills you can learn.

- Mic technique is not difficult to learn. It comes easily with experience.

- Most singers do not know how to sight-sing, but to be able to sight-sing is a useful tool to have. It might also make you more desirable for certain singing jobs.

SECTION FIVE:
MAINTENANCE, BREAKDOWN AND RECOVERY

We use our voices continually – at work, at home, in the bar, in noisy clubs, talking on the phone and, of course, when we sing. Normally our voices work well and rarely let us down. Occasionally, some of us do encounter voice problems, and these are invariably connected to the sorts of things we put our voices through.

Professional voice-users are especially prone to breakdown simply because they use their voices more than others. These people, in particular, will benefit from observing some basic rules of voice care.

Taking on board what I say in this section may well save you a lot of trouble and, for some, help you avoid developing long-term voice problems.

Chapter 20
Voice Care

If you sing regularly it is very important to take good care of your voice. Voice care applies just as much to your speaking voice as it does to your singing voice. Remember, as a singer *you* are your instrument; and your instrument, like any other, needs special care and maintenance.

Do's And Don'ts

Many of the problems singers encounter are caused by what happens outside their actual gigs or rehearsals. Speaking, or more accurately, shouting over loud music is a real strain for most people. Many singers will sing for a few hours with no real problems, and then move on to a noisy club or bar where they then wreck their voices.

Top tip: When speaking over loud music avoid raising the pitch of your voice and keep it low. This will help to prevent you pushing your voice too much. If you try to raise your voice high above the background noise there's a very good chance you'll strain it. Alternatively, some people find it helpful if they make their voices very 'twangy' and nasal. In a noisy environment no one will notice it sounding a bit odd.

I am not going to pull any punches here. If you are a singer DO NOT SMOKE. I know many singers *do* smoke, but aside from negatively affecting your breath control, smoking acts as an irritant. Smoking will also make you more prone to sore throats and coughs. When you cough, your vocal cords collide in a brutal fashion. Be warned. It is often when people have bad coughs and carry on singing that serious vocal problems can arise. Also, over time, smoking changes the make-up of your vocal cords and makes them thicker, more like hard skin!

It follows, therefore, you should try to avoid smoky atmospheres. I suffer terribly if I have been in a smoky environment for any length of time. My voice will always feel rough the next day. These days, of course, singers benefit greatly from the ban on smoking in public places; the poor singers of the past really did suffer.

Throat clearing can set up a cycle of irritation. If you keep clearing your throat you will create mucus and then want to clear it again etc. If you are a throat clearer try to inhibit the urge to clear. Drink water, or you can try to 'fire' the mucus off your cords in a harmless way by making a low 'uh' noise as you pull in your tummy.

One of the best pieces of advice I can give regarding looking after your voice is to drink lots of water – not alcohol! I know it sounds boring and not very rock 'n' roll, but alcohol, as I mentioned before, increases the blood supply to your cords and makes them slightly swollen. If they do become swollen, there is an increased risk of you doing damage. Alcohol also dehydrates you, which is not good for the voice. You may feel a little less anxious after a few drinks but the effect of alcohol on your cords will result in your voice being less reliable than usual. Also with the lack of inhibition you are more likely to overdo things and push your voice. My advice is to save the drinks until after the show. Having said that, I wouldn't personally drink alcohol even then if I had another big show the following day.

A surprising number of people are severely affected by acid reflux; they have to avoid such things as fruit juices, fizzy drinks and tomatoes, otherwise their throats become very sore and their vocal cords swollen. Spicy food is another contributor – sad but true, you curry fans! If you do suffer from acid reflux, try to eat at least two hours before you go to bed. Many voice specialists consider acid reflux one of the major contributory factors behind many voice disorders. If you have continuous reflux problems you should seek medical advice.

Dairy produce is to be avoided; it creates excess mucus and clogs you up. So, sadly, no milkshakes or chocolate bars before you sing. Many people find bananas quite 'clagging' as well.

Drinking a lot of tea or coffee if you are singing is not great either. Herbal teas and warm water are good.

Avoid ice in your drinks prior to singing; it will make your cords contract. Honey is fine and feels soothing on your throat, but it won't repair the damage if you have strained your voice. Don't have too much lemon as it is very acidic. If you drink honey and lemon in hot water, it is the water that will keep you hydrated, but, of course, drinks go into your stomach and not down your airway past your vocal cords. STEAM is the thing that has the most immediate effect.

A steam inhaler can be a godsend for many. You can get these in regular pharmacies/drugstores. The old-fashioned bowl of hot water and towel over the head version is just as good. When you inhale steam the moisture gets right down to your cords and is very soothing. Many singers use steam rooms for the same reason. I recommend steaming two or three times a day if you are experiencing voice problems.

Some people find chewing fresh ginger or drinking ginger tea helpful.

Rest. It may seem obvious, but if your voice is tired or if you have developed problems, the more you can rest your voice the better. When I say rest I mean from talking as well as singing. Try not to talk on the phone excessively, and avoid going anywhere you have to raise your voice. Football games and other sports involving a lot of vocal participation from the audience are out!

The straw exercise (see page 31) is great for voice rehab and getting it back after a lay off. Do it in 5-minute bursts. It doesn't matter how much you do of it, the more the merrier, as long as you're making sure your larynx feels relaxed the whole time. Keep the pitch low if you feel any tightening, and when sirening just descend. It may feel better to use the wide tube into water if your voice is tired.

Regular exercise, eating healthily and keeping fit are all important. Remember, *you* are your instrument, and the more you take care of it the better. Any sort of aerobic exercise is good. If you are working out in the gym, however, be careful if you are doing a lot of weights or sit-ups; it is easy to strain your voice and get tight around your throat area.

Always warm up before you sing – five minutes can be sufficient (I shall be dealing with this in detail in the next chapter).

Practice regularly. You will strengthen your voice and increase your awareness of how you are using it.

DO	DON'T
• Always warm up before singing.	• Start a rehearsal or performance cold.
• Drink water (un-iced) and herbal teas.	• Drink alcohol before singing.
	• Drink fruit juices, fizzy and iced drinks.
	• Eat dairy products, tomatoes, and spicy foods.
• Practice regularly.	• Over-practice.
• Look after your voice in rehearsals.	• Get carried away in rehearsal or sound checks. (Don't sing at full volume all the time.)
• If you speak over loud music, keep the pitch low.	• Speak/shout over loud music.
• Rest your voice if it is tired or you have a cold.	• Cough or clear your throat too vigorously.
• Inhale steam if your voice is tired, you have had a cold, or have been in a smoky environment.	• Smoke. Avoid smoky environments.
• Keep fit and healthy. Get as much sleep as possible.	• Put any strain on the larynx when working out in the gym.

Public Speaking

As well as being a singing coach I also do general voice work with TV presenters and other professional voice-users. I work with them to get the best out of their voices, and my approach is virtually the same as the one I use with singers.

The emphasis is still on the use of the breath, support, resonance, openness, and the importance of having a free body and connecting your body to the sound. It is important to make sure their voices are working efficiently and to iron out any problem areas.

For example, if they are not using the breath properly, their voices will be 'shallow' and may sound 'caught' in their throats – clearly not what you want from a presenter.

Schoolteachers are heavy voice users and many suffer from voice problems. While, hopefully, few teachers these days regularly shout at their pupils, the constant use of their voices, particularly when 'projecting' in front of a class, will soon reveal weaknesses and frailties.

People in various other professions are often required to give talks and presentations that can be vocally demanding. In these contexts there are certain techniques that can be applied which will maximise delivery and help to avoid potential voice problems.

Presentations

Many of the things I say about singing in this book have a direct relevance to normal speech. If you have a presentation or a speech to give, you can practice it using some of the techniques I have already described.

Many people experience a terrible feeling of dread and panic at the thought of making a presentation. If you are one of these, start by using breathing exercises to calm yourself – they will also help you to focus.

As I have already stressed, preparation is the key to good delivery. If you practice the following it will not only vastly improve your confidence but also your delivery.

> *1. Firstly, focus on your breath. Work out where to breathe – you can pencil in breath marks in your text. Rehearse with your hands on your tummy, taking your time and making sure your breath is relaxed, low and not 'snatched'.*
>
> *2. Practice a section, emphasising the vowels. Write it out just like the 'nonsense' writing on page 91. Feel the different places where the vowels resonate.*
>
> *3. Practice and hold a pot on your head with both hands. This will keep your head still and open you up across your chest.*
>
> *4. Practice and swing your arms at the same time. This will really help to open up and relax your body. Also use the 'fencing' arms to open you up and get your voice in touch with your body.*
>
> *5. Rehearse using a mirror, observing your general body use and paying particular attention to how you are standing. Make sure you are open in your body and not slumped or hunched. Work out where you are going to look when you are making your presentation – remember, eye contact is very powerful.*
>
> *6. Work on your delivery. Make sure the pitch is varied and not on a monotone. This is so important because it will help to bring your presentation to life. Listen to how newsreaders and presenters on television and radio do this.*
>
> *7. You need energy in your delivery. On a scale of 1 to 10 you need to be at least 7 to deliver an engaging presentation.*
>
> *8. Practice using visualisation techniques (see page 155).*

Rehearsal Technique

Many singers damage their voices overdoing things in rehearsal. Be sensible and don't over-sing and tire out your voice. If you are singing with a choir, obviously it is not up to you when you take breaks, but don't sing at full throttle for the whole rehearsal. Often a rehearsal will be two to three hours long and your voice will get tired if you are not careful.

If you are rehearsing with a band you have a little more control. However, the rehearsal studio is a potential danger zone for many singers. Don't sing all the time you are rehearsing. Pace yourself and take decent breaks. Don't sing constantly at full volume. Clearly, you want to build up your strength and stamina, but don't push it.

Classical singers protect their voices in rehearsals by 'marking'. This means that they don't sing out fully. For example, they may sing high passages either quietly or an octave down. They do as much as they feel is right at the time, depending on how close they are to their performance.

You might consider doing something similar yourself. If you have got a lot of high material, sing it in your head voice or falsetto, down an octave, or take a lower harmony. Never push the top. If your voice starts to feel tired or strained, stop singing. Also, if the rehearsal is going well and your voice feels good, don't be tempted to keep going until your voice packs up.

A guy I used to teach cancelled his lesson one day as he had overdone it during a rehearsal. I was quite surprised because he was particularly focused, practiced hard and was developing a good technique. I asked him what had happened and he explained that he was singing so well and enjoying himself so much that he got carried away. He was fine for the first five hours, but it was the next three that did him in! I had to laugh.

If you can't hear yourself well you may start to 'push' the sound and this will put pressure on your vocal cords. Some people use headphones and a lot of people use earplugs, or even better, 'in ears', not only to hear themselves better but also for ear protection, which is extremely important. A straightforward way of hearing yourself is to get the rest of the band to turn down. They may take some persuading, but it is for everyone's benefit in the end.

Tour And Gig Survival

If you want to survive regular gigging, touring, long recording stints, or a heavy rehearsal schedule, you need to know how to look after your voice properly (this goes for both lead and backing vocalists). Everything I have said so far about taking care of your voice is relevant.

If you misuse your voice through constantly straining and tightening your throat area, your vocal cords can become swollen and will not meet the way they should. This will result in the sound becoming very breathy or hoarse. More seriously, if this keeps occurring it may result in long-term damage.

As I have said, most strained voices will recover with rest, but this isn't much help if you are in the middle of a tour or the recording of an album. However, there is a lot you can do to avoid straining your voice in the first place.

Using the breath correctly to support your singing is crucial. You need to work the breath and not your throat muscles. Having a good singing technique is the single most important factor in preserving your voice, but consider following a number of basic do's and don'ts.

I have already given you some practical advice on voice care and in the section *Gigging Sound* (page 153) we discussed issues relating to monitors, sound systems and sound people. If, despite everyone's best efforts, you still end up not being able to hear yourself well, try your hardest not to push. It won't help the audience hear any better, and in all likelihood will result in you straining your voice. Change to using your head voice or falsetto more if you are having problems with high stuff.

Drink lots of water (but not iced water or alcohol) before a gig. You should try not to cough or clear your throat too vigorously (it is too abrasive on the cords). In fact, if you have a bad cold or a sore throat, try not to sing – you run the risk of losing your voice for a long period.

DON'T SMOKE! DON'T SMOKE! DON'T SMOKE!

Eating immediately before a gig is not recommended. As we have seen, many singers avoid certain types of food such as dairy products like cheese or chocolate as they find these create too much mucus.

It is all very well, I hear you say, telling us to avoid noisy, smoky, boozy atmospheres, when that is exactly what we would normally expect from the average rock venue (although legislation has been largely successful in removing smoke from the equation these days). I know what you mean; but I am simply suggesting you avoid what you can. It is easy, for example, after a gig with the adrenalin still pumping, to slip into a lot of high-spirited shouting. But you could just as easily train yourself to chill out after a gig and elect not to do this, thereby protecting your voice. Remember, if you find yourself talking a lot, especially if you are having to raise your voice in order to be heard, make you voice nasal or low in your chest and not pushed.

Breakdown And Recovery

If you have persistent voice problems your GP/physician will generally refer you to a voice specialist who will assess the nature of the damage and may take a look at your vocal cords with the help of a laryngoscope. This is a little camera on the end of a probe generally fed in through your nose (yuk!). There are many different types and severity of voice disorder. You may, for example, have a general soreness, or some sort of swelling on your cords caused by misuse. Sometimes these turn out to be cysts, polyps or nodules.

Incidentally, one famous singer I worked with was unlucky enough to have a cyst *inside* one of his cords, which is quite rare (and in this case it seems likely he was born with it). He had it removed by surgery and worked hard to build a good singing technique. Ironically, I think it is the best thing that could have happened to him, as he has had to learn to take care of his voice and use it properly.

Cysts don't always have to be removed, it just depends on where they are and their size.

I have a team of excellent voice specialists and therapists I recommend people to if they have any problems. I have over the years been invited along to several voice clinics to see people have their vocal cords looked at. This has been an invaluable experience and I have seen all sorts of interesting disorders. The most extreme case I ever saw was that of a man who had actually drunk (voluntarily!) battery acid!! Don't ask me why, but needless to say his throat didn't look too pretty!

Professor of Laryngology and Consultant ENT surgeon, Professor Martin Birchall, is a cutting edge expert in his field. I have been lucky enough to sit in on his voice clinics. He is a great educator and enthusiast and he is continually doing all sorts of ground-breaking research and surgery – amongst many other amazing things, he has even transplanted a larynx. Martin has taught me so much about the voice and the problems people can have. I am very grateful to him for his continued support and advice.

Nodules

Nodules are the most common lesions that can develop on your vocal cords (folds). They are very rarely larger than 1.5 mm in diameter and are non-malignant. They are a bit like calluses and are formed by trauma arising from contact between opposite surfaces of the vocal cords. They are usually symmetrical, with one on each cord. Very occasionally sufferers will just have one.

Generally these days, nodules are treated (and eliminated) using a combination of speech therapy and, if you are a singer, learning to sing with good technique and breath support. Surgery is rare and is only necessary if the nodules have become hard. Many people will get rid of them completely through good vocal practice, so if you *are* unfortunate enough to develop nodules, don't lose heart. If you have avoided them so far, follow the advice above and keep it that way.

The difficulty with voice disorders is that you can get into a vicious circle with them. Often it can start with laryngitis, a bad cough, or an infection resulting in lots of throat-clearing. All these things can leave your vocal cords sore and swollen. If you then sing, your poor cords don't stand a chance. The best advice is not to sing if you have got a bad cold or sore throat as you risk permanent damage.

Of course, many problems arise purely as a result of poor voice use, including excessive shouting at sports games or over loud music, and 'pushing' your voice in a harmful way when singing. As you begin to experience vocal problems you will often have to push or force more to get the sound out. This makes the problem even worse, which is why it is crucial to spot difficulties early on and deal with them.

I have worked with many singers who either have or have had nodules. I usually know when someone has nodules before they tell me – and before they know themselves in some cases. There are a number of tell-tale signs (however, these symptoms on their own are not always definitive evidence of the existence of nodules): as a rule, a singer with nodules will find that their voice is particularly husky in the mornings and takes a long time to warm up. Some people's voices will be permanently husky. For some time they may feel a general soreness after strenuous voice use.

If you have always sung in tune and then begin to experience problems with pitching notes, this can be an indicator as well. You may find your voice has become lower in pitch. This is a result of the increased mass of the vocal cords, which will vibrate at a lower frequency than usual.

Nodules can also make you produce a very breathy tone due to the fact that your vocal cords won't meet properly, allowing extra air to escape with the sound. It can be so breathy and weak in the upper middle part of your voice that the sound almost disappears.

Another common problem associated with nodules is the inability to sing at medium volumes: you may find you can sing only at the extremes (very quietly or full belt) and that nothing much happens in between.

Some people present just one or two of the above symptoms; others display pretty much all of them.

If you are experiencing any of these problems on a frequent basis I suggest you get referred to a medical voice specialist. Only an expert can tell you exactly what is causing your problems – the symptoms I have described may be no real cause for concern, but could be evidence of various forms of voice disorder.

It is only if your nodules harden that you are likely to need surgery. It is preferable to avoid surgery if at all possible since, if you are unlucky, you may end up with scar tissue on your cords. This may well affect your singing, as your cords are unlikely to meet in the same way they did before.

It is essential that you learn to look after yourself properly if you have had nodules (or any other voice disorder), whether you have had surgery or not, because if you continue with the same pattern of abuse they may recur.

The section on voice care will help you learn to look after your voice properly. If you keep your voice healthy and develop a good singing technique, you are unlikely to encounter vocal problems, leaving you free to enjoy a lifetime of trouble-free singing.

I want to emphasise that the most severe vocal problems are very rare and it is easy to become paranoid every time you get a sore throat. If you learn to use your voice healthily you can be pretty confident you'll avoid any nasties!

On The Mend

Speech therapists tackle all types of voice disorders. Much of their work is with professional voice users such as public speakers, actors, teachers, presenters, telephone-users, and, of course, singers.

They start by teaching good vocal hygiene, which I have been through elsewhere in this book.

Sometimes complete voice rest is recommended for certain problems, but, as I keep emphasising, you must learn to use your voice properly if the symptoms are not to return.

A speech therapist will help you develop a good general vocal technique – normally focusing on the speaking voice. They teach many of the aspects of technique outlined in this book such as breathing and support, vowel formation and resonance, and good body use.

Getting it right obviously takes practice. It takes time to get your muscles working in the right way, especially if you have slipped into some bad vocal habits. Learning to use your voice correctly may mean you will never need another visit to the speech therapist or doc.

Working Environment

Many working environments contribute to voice strain. This is particularly true of jobs that demand excessive voice use, or those that require you constantly to raise your voice.

Passive smoking used to be a huge problem for singers. Thankfully with smoking being banned in most public spaces in the UK and Ireland and in an increasing number of countries around the world (including parts of the USA), singers are more and more able to avoid the threat posed by smoky working environments. Working in smoky atmospheres is bad for you and particularly bad for your voice. If you do find yourself in a situation where you cannot avoid inhaling smoke I would recommend regular steaming.

When I left university, in order to subsidise the (initially meagre!) income I earned through singing, I did a telesales job for some time. I found the constant talking on the phone a real strain on my voice, and this was starting to have an adverse effect on my singing. I was fortunate enough to have a sympathetic boss who agreed to let me move to the admin department instead.

CHAPTER 20 SUMMARY

- It is important to follow basic principles of voice care in order to keep your voice healthy and working well. See the Do's and Don'ts table on page 175.

- Be careful about what you eat and drink, and watch out for signs of acid reflux.

- Many people are heavy voice users at work. Just like singers, these people will also benefit from learning about breath, support, resonance, openness and having a free body.

- Those having to give a talk or presentation may wish to prepare themselves using the suggestions given in this chapter.

- Rehearsing your material thoroughly is very important, but guard against overdoing things as you will make your voice tired and run the risk of losing it.

- Those on long tours must take extra care with their voices. Having a good singing technique is the most important factor, but singers should also look after their voices in between gigs.

- Excessive voice misuse and strain can lead to a general soreness or some sort of swelling on your cords.

- Rest and the use of steam are the only real remedies for voice loss and swollen cords.

- Do the straw exercise for voice rehab.

- Serious physical problems affecting singers are not common and even nodules rarely require surgery these days.

- Nodules are now more commonly treated with a combination of good vocal hygiene, speech therapy and, if you are a singer, good singing lessons.

- If you have had problems, you must learn to use your voice properly if the symptoms are not to return.

- If you are serious about your singing, you may have to consider avoiding certain working environments.

Chapter 21
Warm-Up

There is a difference between practicing singing exercises and warming up. The word *exercise* suggests a workout and that is what singing exercises are designed to do. They are for strengthening and gaining more control over your voice. When you warm up your voice you are *not* doing a workout; you are simply warming it up in readiness to sing. As we have already stated, warming up your voice before singing is very important.

Warm-ups are usually quite short: the last thing you want is to tire out your voice before you start. Warming up your voice, however, will take longer on some days than it does on others. It will all depend on how tired you are, if you have been drinking, had a late night, or spent time in a smoky atmosphere. If you have been overdoing things vocally, your voice will also feel harder to 'start up'.

It is advisable to get your voice going a few hours before you sing. If your voice is not feeling great you could start by having a steam before warming up. However, you don't need to do your warm-up all in one go.

'The straw/tube' is a great way to start the day as it is so portable. Many singers I work with do it in the shower and while getting dressed; in this way they'll have done a decent warm up before they even leave the house, so their voice will be ready to go whatever they are doing.

Luciano Pavarotti, *the* master of singing technique used to warm up in short bursts on the day of a performance. He would sleep in until about 11.00 or 12.00 o'clock. When he woke up he would sing immediately for a few minutes. After 'breakfast' he would then sing for about fifteen minutes. He had another burst of five minutes before he went to the venue, and another five minutes before going on stage.

Why Do A Warm-Up?

If you were going to play sport, go for a jog, or do a dance class, you would always do some sort of warm-up or stretching beforehand, or at least at the beginning of a session. When you are taking part in sport you are often using muscles in ways they are not normally used. Stretching and loosening up reduces the likelihood of damage and also helps to maximise your performance. Singing also involves specific muscle use and so a warm-up has the same importance.

Warming up does what it says. Your voice will feel smoother, more open and resonant, more flexible and probably louder. If you never warm up before singing there is a risk of both short term and long term damage.

Always warm up before you sing, whether it is for a choir or band rehearsal, gig or soundcheck. You need to make time for it, even if it has to be in the shower or in the car on the way to the venue. You run the risk of damaging your voice more easily if you sing 'cold'. Furthermore, your vocal performance is almost guaranteed to be poorer as a result.

The vast majority of successful artists with whom I have worked, warm up their voices religiously before a performance. Some do it individually and others have established a routine with their band members and backing singers. One artist who comes to mind as having learned the importance of this is the very talented and charismatic John Newman. John will never go on stage without warming up properly. He has found this is an important part of getting the most out of his performance as well as enabling him to keep his voice going during long periods of touring.

As I have said, you don't need to do a long warm-up – about 10 to 15 minutes will do for most people. Don't make it an extensive vocal workout; if the warm-up becomes vocally tiring, this is obviously counter-productive.

When you warm up you need to get your whole voice going. Obviously, there are many different ways of doing this – one, for example, would be to base your warm-up around your favourite singing exercises. You can download some warm-up exercises from my website.

Warm-Up Exercises

You can warm up your voice in a number of different ways. You could select some of your favourite singing exercises from the ones I have given you, but be careful not to push. You should aim to get your voice open, connected to the support, and resonating.

If the exercises don't suit you, try other warm-ups. If you are warming up your voice for speech or singing, the following are all good.

The first one is a favourite of mine.

---

1. Hang down to the floor like a rag doll, with either straight legs or knees slightly bent – whichever is more comfortable. Let your head and arms hang and your neck be free. Breathe in and out through your nose. Hum a single note, fairly low in your voice – wherever it feels good. The note will last for as long as the breath lasts. Feel it resonating in your back. Repeat five times.

2. Put your hands on your waist, bring your head up so that it is in line with your spine, breathe in and come up to standing. Let your arms hang loosely by your sides and repeat the humming, this time concentrating on the sound resonating in your chest. Do this five times.

3. Remain standing. Repeat the humming, imagining the resonance is coming into the front of your face around your sinuses. It may help to raise the pitch of the hum. (Rest your fingers lightly on the front of your face to feel the resonance.)

4. Stay standing. Place your hands on the back of your head. Repeat the humming, thinking of the resonance buzzing in the back of your head.

5. Let your arms hang loosely by your sides. Now hum and imagine all those resonances joining up from the base of your spine, up your back, into the back of your head, over the top of your head, into the front of your face, then chest, and down into your tummy.

This is a great warm-up and one that really gets you in touch with the different areas in your body where you can resonate the sound. If you do this with your eyes closed it may be more powerful.

Singing long, held notes on any vowel you like is another good warm-up. Choose mid-range to low notes.

'Sirening' is also useful. As well as doing it on 'vv' you can sing it on an 'ng' sound rather than an 'mm'. You produce the 'ng' sound right at the front of your face, behind your nose. You need to open your mouth as you go higher. Sirening encourages a good jaw position (but be careful not to tense your tongue).

> *Start at the bottom of your voice and slide right up to the top as high as you can go, and then all the way down. You can also try going from high to low. You will sound a bit like a cat or an emergency vehicle siren, but try not to be self-conscious – despite what people say! The idea is to do this completely smoothly with no gear changes, which can be quite tricky. If your voice 'jumps' try placing the sound more forward in the front of your face and top of your head. Being able to achieve this is a sign of a healthy voice.*

Always check to make sure your body isn't tense when you are warming up or doing exercise. You could try some arm swinging or some other body-freeing exercises.

> *A good warm-up to get your lips, teeth and tongue going is to say the words 'chocolate' and 'minim'. Walk around the room swinging your arms saying 'chocolate' (clearly emphasising each syllable) as many times as you can in one breath. Vary the pitch of it, going higher and lower. Repeat this several times. Then do the same on the word 'minim'. This makes the front of your mouth, lips, teeth and tongue more 'alive' and ready for action.*

CHAPTER 21 SUMMARY

- You should always do some kind of warm-up before you sing.

- Like other kinds of physical activity, singing involves specific muscle use and so a warm-up has the same importance.

- Suggestions for ways of warming up are given in this chapter.

Chapter 22
Singing Lessons

Do I Need Singing Lessons?

This is a very good question. Obviously I would say yes – although it depends with whom! Undoubtedly, everyone can benefit from good vocal tuition, but there are, I'm afraid, a lot of vocal coaches out there whose teaching you need like a hole in the head. Bad singing instruction can range from downright useless to actively damaging. But before I get on my high horse about those responsible, let's talk about the positive effects of good singing coaching,

All types of people come to me for lessons, from top professionals wishing to hone their skills, to people who sing purely for fun and are curious about their own potential. Some people use it as a form of relaxation or 'therapy' as they can really lose themselves in their singing.

I have no doubts about the beneficial effects of singing, both at a physical and emotional level. There is evidence, for example, that it raises your endorphins. Put simply, it's good for you; it makes you feel better!

Different people, as we have said, will be aiming to take their singing to different levels. You may want to be able to sing purely for your own personal enjoyment, perform a song at a party, impress on Karaoke night, sing in a local choir, play a leading role in your local operatic society, or front a rock band. Whatever your aspirations, good singing lessons can help you achieve them.

Some people have lessons if they are preparing for an audition. Others may have joined a drama group and need to get their confidence up. In fact, there are endless reasons for people to start singing lessons.

It's exciting when you start to explore your voice. I love the fact that everyone's voice is unique. I get a buzz from hearing someone's voice for the first time and working out exactly what they need to do to improve their singing.

Some people have lessons to prove to themselves (and others!) that they can actually hold a tune. They are often adults who at an early age were told they couldn't sing or were hopelessly 'tone deaf'. As I said earlier, everyone can learn to sing in tune given time; I haven't had a failure yet! It gives people such a feeling of happiness and satisfaction to achieve what they and others always believed was impossible. Learning to sing in tune in my experience is a significant issue for a surprisingly large number of people.

Some singers, sadly, only come when they are experiencing difficulties. Maybe they have started singing with a band and are struggling in rehearsals.

Very experienced singers also have lessons to keep on top of their technique and to make sure their voices stay in good shape. It doesn't matter how good you are, it is easy to get a bit sloppy and fall into bad habits. It can be vey useful to have someone else's 'ears' listening to you, checking everything is okay, and looking for areas that can be improved. Others can often hear things about your singing that you don't hear yourself.

You can never stop learning and improving. I am still learning new things about singing all the time, and I want it to stay that way!

What Happens In A Singing Lesson?

Singing lessons vary and every teacher will have a different style and slightly different approach or emphasis.

In a typical lesson I would cover breathing and voice exercises as well as working on a song. The exercises would take more or less the first half of the lesson. When working on the song I would make sure the singer was singing it technically well, focusing on breath, support, resonance, body use and awareness, as well as style and phrasing.

However, if someone were working on a piece for an imminent performance, audition or recording, I would do a short warm-up and spend more time on the pieces being sung.

Some teachers are good technicians and spend most of the lesson time on technique and not much on repertoire. Personally, I like to pay proper attention to both.

Some singing coaches only deal with interpretation and phrasing and don't work on sound production and technique. Such coaches are often excellent pianists. Many classical singers use these in addition to their singing lessons to help them learn repertoire.

When learning repertoire thoroughly you need to practice with the appropriate accompaniment. If you are preparing for an audition or recital, a few sessions with a good accompanist/coach is a great way of rehearsing.

What Makes A Good Teacher?

I strongly believe most singers would benefit from some knowledge of good vocal technique. A good teacher should have a thorough knowledge of how the voice works and be able to convey it in simple, understandable language. I also believe they should be experienced singers themselves.

As a general rule, never be bullied into doing anything in a lesson that makes your voice feel very uncomfortable or results in you developing a sore throat. Sometimes when you are working on technique you may be focusing on loosening your tongue or jaw, for example, and you may experience some tension or tightness in that area. If this happens, discuss it with your teacher – don't just keep quiet.

Your teacher should be able to give you things to prevent this from happening. If not, they should stop that particular exercise and try something different. If your voice is repeatedly getting sore or tired in your lessons (assuming there are no underlying physical problems), frankly, you should change teachers.

Sometimes your voice may get tired when you are practicing or having a lesson due to the material you are singing. Some singers insist on singing material that is too high or 'pushy' for them. As you develop your technique through practice it will become easier to sing higher without straining.

I have taught plenty of singers who, after several months of hard work, were able to do their rehearsals and gigs without vocal strain. You need to start gradually and build up. Don't sing too high for too long as you will simply get vocally tired.

Frequently, when singers start working on their technique they find they can keep it going for a while, but then their support muscles stop working. Furthermore, the more they sing, the more the old tensions have a tendency to creep back. The idea, then, is to work on material in short bursts and gradually build up stamina.

Personality is important. Your teacher should feel approachable, and there should be some rapport. This doesn't mean you have to be best friends, but you certainly need to feel at ease with them for it to work.

I am not a great fan of 'methods'. Some such as the Estill Method, for example, have become very popular. One problem is that it has become common for people to go on short training courses in certain 'methods' and then believe they can teach singing by simply applying the 'rules' they have learned as if it were that simple. In my experience 'methods' are open to misinterpretation and confusion. As a consequence, I am often left to pick up the pieces. I believe in a more holistic approach, combining both the individual physical and emotional characteristics of the singer.

Bad Teachers

Unfortunately, there are many singing teachers out there who are not merely ineffective, but are, through the things they teach, actually causing damage to people's voices. Sadly, I've had personal experience of several such teachers over the years and, as a result, feel very strongly about the subject.

My first complaint against the poorest teachers I have encountered is that they had an inability to hear where I had technical difficulties. Secondly, they pressured me into doing things with my voice it really didn't want to do.

I think as a singer you should trust your instincts. If you are given something to do that really doesn't feel right then don't do it. I appreciate this is not always as easy as it sounds: you tend to trust your teacher, and it can be hard to question their authority.

In my case, I was very focused and therefore practiced very hard. Unhappily, this just reinforced the bad practices I was being taught and made things even worse. I look back on this now and know that at the time I felt quite uneasy about some of the things I was asked to do. But as I was, and still am, passionate about singing I practiced hard – very hard. The trouble was, as I said, I was practicing totally the wrong kinds of things. At the time I wasn't to know.

The only good thing about having experienced so much bad teaching is that I had to work through all that I had been taught and sort out the good stuff from the rubbish. By painstakingly doing so I feel I have arrived at a thorough understanding of what comprises good practice. I hope, as a result, this process has made me a better teacher, although, as I said earlier, you never stop learning.

I have heard a number of horror stories over the years relating to singing teachers. Some derive from personal experience; others have been related to me by singers with whom I have worked.

I know of one well-known teacher of rock & pop singers, for example, who starts by playing a recording of a singer doing vocal exercises. The poor student is then expected to join in and sing along without any intervention or tuition. This is incredibly lazy; if a teacher does this they aren't properly engaged with the lesson and won't be able to hear clearly what you are doing. Consequently they won't know what it is you need to work on.

It is vital that the exercises are tailored to individual needs since no two singers are the same. I constantly stop during exercises to draw attention to different aspects of technique – vowel formation, breath, support, resonance, placing, registers, etc.

The last I heard, this particular teacher gives little or no instruction as to how to do the exercises, and doesn't stop the 'backing' if the exercises are too high or out of range. He has even been known to text or check his emails while the singer is struggling their way through the exercises! Appalling.

As I have already mentioned, occasionally singers are taught to sing their material exclusively using a mic. Sure, practicing with a mic has its place, but if you only ever sing like this you will never develop any depth to your voice or decent technique. You will be left with a shallow voice lacking resonance, tone and support.

Classical singing teachers are not immune to charges of incompetence either. Most will have studied singing extensively, but I'm afraid many lack a sound knowledge of technique and a proper understanding of the mechanics of the voice.

The fact that someone is a good singer doesn't necessarily guarantee they will be a good teacher of singing. Many are just plain ineffective – neither good nor bad, but others will really do damage. All my teachers were classical singers, and I have been taught many weird and wonderful things down the line. One teacher used a technique that involved almost 'shouting' the notes as high as I possibly could. The idea was to get you in touch with your emotional centre and place the voice where you speak. This was a nightmare for me: it always hurt and she often reduced me to tears in the lesson.

Another teacher I had whilst studying music at university totally failed to hear I wasn't singing with enough upper resonance or head voice and that I was really pushing the top of my voice. I was singing very high repertoire at the time and I had a huge amount of tension in my jaw – in fact it used to seize up as I was singing! She did nothing to help me. My breath control became hopeless as I always forced the sound. The only thing that saved me was that my degree course finished and I didn't have to study with her any more.

'Excessive talking' (to put it politely) is another problem among some teachers. Now, I like a good chat myself, and I enjoy very much the social side of getting to know the people with whom I'm working, but I build this into my teaching schedule as 'spill-over' time. Unfortunately some teachers don't do this. Some 'like the sound of their own voices'. They spend so much of the lesson sharing stories about whom they have taught and what they have done they end up doing very little actual teaching. I know a famous teacher of West End show singers who can spend as much as 45 minutes of a one-hour lesson talking, leaving only 15 minutes for actual teaching! Well, if you find that acceptable, that is up to you. I wouldn't put up with it personally, especially as some of these charlatans are charging a fortune for their services.

Avoid teachers who appear to adopt what feels like a negative or unsupportive approach. One teacher, after listening to me sing for the first time, commented rather disparagingly, "Well, I suppose your voice is *usable!*". I was at the time working as a professional singer. I may have had a few technical problems, but people always seemed to like the sound I made. Fortunately, I had strong self-belief and swiftly moved on to another teacher. I don't know what her problem was, or if she knew anything about technique (although I suspect not), but the issue with teachers who are actively discouraging and negative is that they can shatter a singer's confidence and literally put them off for life.

In contrast, I strongly believe in taking a positive approach and consequently use a lot of encouragement and praise wherever possible. There is never any excuse for being unkind or patronising – or sycophantic either for that matter. Interestingly, there are some artists who will only ever go to singing coaches of the 'ego-massage' variety, regardless of how useless they might be from a technical point of view. I know of some successful 'media' singing coaches who are excellent at buttering people up, but if you scratch below the surface you will find only a very patchy knowledge of technique. I refer to these coaches as the 'style over substance' brigade.

The proof of the pudding, as they say, is in the eating. If a singing coach is worth their salt (assuming you have a willing singer), then you should see a marked improvement in the singing pretty quickly. The history of singing coaching has always been marked by accusations (often justified) of charlatanism. I say, if you are doing everything your singing coach is telling you to do and practicing conscientiously, but you still don't experience any obvious progress, then it's time you changed your singing coach.

Finally, be suspicious of people who say they don't take beginners. In my experience this is usually because they don't know enough about technique and wouldn't know where to start, or that it is simply 'beneath them'. I'm afraid I find myself questioning the motivation behind these people wanting to become singing teachers in the first place. As far as I'm concerned, if someone is keen to work on their voice then I am too, whatever level they happen to be. I enjoy the challenge of different voices and the 'problem-solving' side of things – figuring out the areas that need to be worked on in order to get the absolute best out of their singing.

I love my singing coaching and try always to achieve the highest possible standards. I feel very lucky to earn my living this way. Furthermore, I have met a lot of wonderful people over the years through my work, many of whom have become close personal friends.

CHAPTER 22 SUMMARY

- Every singer can benefit from good vocal tuition, but caution should be exercised when choosing a singing teacher.

- You should avoid singing coaches who appear to have a negative or discouraging attitude to your singing, or who you suspect lack real understanding of technique and how your voice works.

- Be wary of 'style over substance' teachers who spend too much time talking about themselves or flattering you in their lessons.

- The kinds of things to look for in a singing teacher are discussed in this chapter.

Afterword
My Top Ten Singers

I am often asked who my favourite singers are and why. It's a very tricky question to answer – like having to select your Desert Island Discs. Because I like singers for all kinds of reasons, it makes reducing my choice down to ten almost impossible. One singer may have a fantastic technique, or a particular tonal quality; another's phrasing or delivery of lyrics may stand them apart. Some singers will captivate due to sheer musicality.

A Top Ten, by its very nature, is always going to be a personal, idiosyncratic thing and my choices won't be everyone's cup of tea. I have, however, tried to explain what it is I like about each of the singers I've singled out. Having limited myself to just ten I am also inevitably forced to omit some real favourites. Furthermore, since I have settled on ten very different singers I am going to have to add the proviso 'in no specific order' to the choices in my list.

It might be fun – and interesting – to analyse your own vocal Top Ten in this way; you often don't know what it is you especially like about a singer until you take the time to think about it.

Luciano Pavarotti

Top of my list for flawless technique has to be Luciano Pavarotti. Whether or not you like opera singers, you can't fail to admire his control and power. Even if you never listen to opera, virtually everyone is familiar with his rendition of *Nessun Dorma*. His voice is so even and balanced. He appears to sing with the whole of his body (and there was plenty of it!) and has an incredibly well-supported voice. When he soars away on his top Cs he keeps his head and body very still; you can see him drawing everything in and down.

I also love the bright resonance in his voice – there is a real 'ring' to it. The placing of the sound is forward in his face and head, but he also has a very open throat, which adds so much power to his singing. You are aware of no obvious change in tone when he moves from chest to head voice. His *passagio* (the transition area between chest to head voice) is so beautifully blended.

Pavarotti made so many excellent recordings, but one album to check out is *King Of The High C's* if you want to hear some scintillating singing!

Kurt Elling

Outside the classical world my all-time favourite is the jazz singer Kurt Elling. He can sing anything. He has the most awesome technique and sings with so much emotion. He has an incredible (four-octave) range and knows his voice inside-out.

His lower register has the timbre of a cello and when he sings there it makes me cry. I have seen him sing many times and had the great pleasure of meeting him after one gig when I couldn't resist telling him this. "You should get out more, lady!" (said kindly, with a smile) was his predictably warm and self-effacing response.

Kurt's live performances are spellbinding; if you get the chance to see him, take it. His scatting is wildly ambitious but incredibly accurate and he sings with such swing. Check him out singing *Nature Boy* with the Sydney Symphony Orchestra on YouTube for a taste of what this amazing singer can do.

His legato singing is particularly beautiful; he conveys so much tenderness and emotion. His version of *In The Wee Small Hours* from the album *Nightmoves* (full track entitled *Leaving/In The Wee Small Hours*) is totally sublime and one of the best, tear-jerking vocals I have ever heard.

Kurt is a master of his craft. He is extremely knowledgeable about jazz music, and his deep love of it is clear for all to see. He is a consummate professional and a superb singer in every way.

Stevie Wonder

The great Stevie Wonder is my next choice. He is another singer who is totally in command of his voice. There is so much power and emotion in his sound. His voice is a very flexible instrument. In fact, listen to his harmonica playing; it is so much like his singing. He bends notes and varies vibrato, constantly changing the 'colour' of his singing.

Above all else, he has such an uplifting, happy-sounding voice. His tone is very bright and you can virtually hear his smile in the sound. Think of the 'la, la, la' section in *My Cherie Amour*; it is so a joyful and inspiring.

The singing is always effortless and so well controlled. His phrasing and feel are superb and his vocals exude so much excitement and energy, whilst retaining tremendous line. He is without doubt a singer who gets in the groove. He also has a very agile voice and is brilliant at scatting and really fast 'licks'.

Stevie has written and sung so many great songs over the years such as *'Superstition'*, *'Signed, Sealed, Delivered, I'm Yours'*, *'I Wish,'* *'You And I'*, *'You Are The Sunshine Of My Life'*, *'Lately'*… and the list goes on. It is impossible to pick a stand-out – they are all brilliant.

Frank Sinatra

Frank Sinatra would probably be on most people's list of great singers. Apart from anything else, he is the supreme *phraser*.

There are so many great songs uniquely associated with him: *'Chicago'*, *'New York, New York'*, *'The Lady Is A Tramp'*, *'Mack The Knife'*, *'Come Fly With Me'*, and, of course, *'My Way'*. My absolute favourite has to be *'It Was A Very Good Year'*. His interpretation of this song is wonderful; the meaning he puts into the words is almost tangible.

The tone of Sinatra's voice is rich and warm and his phrasing is out of this world. Not only does he have such a listenable tone and smooth delivery, but his *timing* is pure genius. Although 'Old Blue Eyes' was a master of the classic ballad, this was a guy who also really knew how to swing!

Eva Cassidy

For emotional intensity my vote has to go to the late great Eva Cassidy. She has a golden voice and uses so many different colours and textures when she sings. She could swing between a full tone with a lot of power and a deeply moving, intense fragility.

She was completely at one with her instrument (acoustic guitar) when she played and I believe that may be at the root of her wonderful musicality.

Her singing is totally transfixing. She was someone who completely made a song her own. In fact, to my view, she brought a whole new meaning to the term 'cover version', blowing everybody else out of the water. There are very few people who can cover classics successfully. Her version of *Over The Rainbow* reduces me to tears every time.

Maria Callas

Someone else who sang with extraordinary emotion was the famous soprano Maria Callas. In my opinion she is unrivalled in the world of opera. She sang with such intense passion and drama, drawing out every last nuance of meaning from both the words and music.

She used a wonderful variety of tone and colour, and her voice is incredibly thrilling and moving. Her magnetic stage presence is legendary, but for those of us unlucky never to have seen her in the flesh, her recordings certainly capture her magic.

Callas was the complete artist and supreme musician, famed for complete devotion to her art. It is difficult to sum up in a few words what is so great about her singing – it's beyond words in a way.

One of my favourite recordings is of the aria *Vissi d'arte* from Puccini's *Tosca* (La Scala, Milan 1953). The range of tone and expression she uses is quite breathtaking. She varies the weight of her voice and musical line to add to the drama. An extraordinary singer and performer.

Ella Fitzgerald

Ella Fitzgerald is another on my all-time-greats list. She is well known as one of the great jazz scatters. Her voice has tremendous agility and can really soar. Her evenness of tone when she moves from one part of her voice to another is staggering. She could literally sing the phone book and make it sound good.

It is, however, her recordings with the guitarist Joe Pass that have a special place in my affections. When they played together there was a seemingly symbiotic relationship, with one playing off the other. They produced a beautifully intimate sound, and generally speaking, I think the jazz electro-acoustic guitar perfectly complements the voice.

Their recording of the Billy Strayhorn classic *Lush Life* is one of my great favourites. Again, Ella's tone is so silky smooth and her singing always sounds completely effortless.

Aretha Franklin

Aretha Franklin has to be one of the most exciting singers of all time. She is known by many as the 'Queen of Soul' and soul she certainly has – by the bucket load. She has huge power in her voice and pushes it to its limits. There is great energy and commitment in her singing, and the more you listen to her, the more excitement builds up inside you.

Her tone is incredibly bright and ringing, and there is a real intensity and focus in her singing. She is completely 'on it' in terms of phrasing. She can throw her voice around wherever she likes, often bending it and using it like an instrument. I love the energetic intensity of her classic hit *Respect* and the great soulful feel of her version of *Natural Woman*.

Thom Yorke

I am a huge fan of Tom Yorke. I love both his plaintive tone and his unconventional approach to singing. His voice has an intoxicating, emotional intensity and fragility. He sings so musically with beautiful line, drawing everything out of every phrase he sings; he almost leans into the phrases. I remember hearing *Paranoid Android,* from the ground-breaking album *OK Computer,* for the first time and being completely blown away.

There are so many exceptional songs to choose from but a particular favourite of mine is *Weird Fishes/Arpeggi* from the album *In Rainbows.* The tone is so haunting; it completely grabs you emotionally and it has a wonderful build. The soaring counter melody adds to the extraordinary beauty of this track.

Take 6

This is a bit of a cheat as, clearly, there are six of them! The reason I have included Take 6 in my list of favourites is that this American Gospel group have taken *a cappella* singing to another level. Their arrangements and choice of harmonies are sublime. The way they phrase together, change dynamics and blend their voices is mind-blowing.

I know I have already mentioned the song *Get Away Jordan* (from the album *Take 6*) but you just have to listen to it. I find it hard to believe six singers can sing so well together. They truly use their voices as instruments, providing all their own percussion and bass parts with their voices alone. In places they sound like a brass section. If you want to feel instantly uplifted, give them a listen.

As I have suggested, inevitably when you write any 'best of' list you will always get people saying, 'but what about him!' and 'how could you leave out her!'. Choosing my *final* ten was in the end almost random, but hopefully they highlight many different aspects of good singing.

If my list hadn't been limited to ten I would definitely have wanted to say something about (in alphabetical order!): Jeff Buckley, Karen Carpenter, Caruso, Jose Carreras, Ray Charles, Kurt Cobain, Nat King Cole, Placido Domingo, Nick Drake, Judy Garland, Marvyn Gaye, Billie Holiday, Mahalia Jackson, Mick Jagger, John Lennon, Paul McCartney, Joni Mitchell, Leontyne Price, Robert Plant, Bonnie Raitt, Otis Redding, Diana Ross, Sting, Bryn

Terfyl, Steven Tyler, Tina Turner. But even then, of course, there would be scores of others.

And finally ...

If you have always wanted to improve your singing, I hope this book has inspired you to do something about it. Follow the basic advice in these pages and keep working at the exercises. Be inspired, and don't give up, be passionate and find *your* voice!

Good luck

Jo Thompson

www.jothompson.net

Further Reading

Communicate With Charisma (Tom Bruno Magdich and Jo Thompson)
ISBN: 978 178299 819 8

The Alexander Technique Workbook (Richard Brennan)
Element Books Ltd
ISBN: 1 8791 025 7

The Voice And Its Disorders (Greene and Mathieson)
Whurr Publishers Ltd
ISBN: 1 86156 196 2

Great Singers On Great Singing (Jerome Hines)
Limelight Editions, New York
ISBN: 0 87910 025 7

It's Your Life, What Are You Going To Do With It?: Make Real Changes In Your Life (Anthony Grant and Jane Greene)
Momentum
ISBN: 1 843 04013 1

Yoga For You (Tara Fraser)
Duncan Baird Publishers, Londonßß
ISBN: 1 904292 27 5

Glossary

A Cappella

Unaccompanied

Alexander Technique

A technique to re-coordinate the body and inhibit misuse.

Baritone

Male voice type, weightier than tenor.

Range: 2nd G below Middle C to high G sharp.

Bass

Lowest male voice type.

Range: 2nd F below Middle C to G above Middle C.

Bass baritone

A male voice with a voice quality lighter than a bass.

Range: Low F to high F sharp.

The belt

Pushing the chest voice very high.

The break

The point at which the chest voice can be pushed no higher and the sound changes to pure head voice (undesirable).

Cadenza

A brilliant or virtuoso passage for solo instrument or voice.

Castrato

A male singer castrated before reaching puberty.

Contralto

The lowest female voice type.

Range: D below Middle C to 2nd B flat above Middle C.

Countertenor

Classical male singer who sings using mainly falsetto.

Chest resonance

Vibration of the singing sound felt in the chest.

Clavicular breathing

Shallow breathing. Breath drawn into the area around the top of the chest and collarbones.

Covering

Modifying the vowel sounds as you sing higher. All vowels become more of a 'yawny' 'awe' sound, sung with an 'open throat'.

Diaphragm

A dome-shaped area of muscle that separates your heart and lungs from the rest of your insides. The main muscle involved in breathing.

Diaphragmatic breathing

Breathing that concentrates on the movement of the diaphragm as a means of control.

Dynamics

Variations in volume musicians use for emotional or dramatic effect.

Falsetto

The highest part of a man's voice – the 'choirboy' part.

Forward resonance

Resonance produced at the front of the face and head.

The 'groove'

The small cavity on either side of your cheeks.

Head Resonance

Vibration of the singing sound felt in your head.

Intercostal breathing

A pattern of breathing that concentrates on the intercostal muscles surrounding your ribcage.

Larynx

Voice box

Legato

Smooth and connected.

Low larynx

Keeping the larynx in a low, relaxed position.

Lip synching

Miming to a pre-recorded vocal track.

Marking

Not singing at full volume in rehearsal.

Mezzo soprano

A female singer whose voice is weightier than a soprano but lighter than a contralto.

Range: F below Middle C to 2nd B above Middle C.

Nodules

Small non-malignant lesions on the vocal cords.

Open throat

Singing with an open 'yawny' space in the back of your throat.

Perfect pitch

The ability to recognise or name a note on first hearing.

Pharynx

The back wall of the throat.

Register

The range of a voice or an instrument.

Relative pitch

The ability to pitch notes from a given starting note.

Resonance

The amplification and alteration of the basic vocal sound by certain areas of the body.

Sight singing

The ability to sing music from a printed score without having previously rehearsed it.

Soft palate

The soft part at the back of the roof of your mouth.

Soprano

Highest female voice type.

Range: G below Middle C up to high C (and beyond).

Support

The control of the breath as you sing.

Tenor

Highest male voice type.

Range: C below Middle C to C above Middle C.

Tessitura

A term used to describe the range of a voice or piece of music in relation to the normal range. If a song is said to have a high *tessitura*, most notes would lie quite high.

Trachea

Windpipe.

Vibrato

The vibration of the singing sound.

Vocal cords/folds

Two pieces of delicate elastic tissue reaching from the back to the front of the larynx.

Index:

Printed in Great Britain
by Amazon.co.uk, Ltd.,
Marston Gate.